At Issue

Interracial Relationships

Other books in the At Issue series:

At Issue

Interracial Relationships

David M. Haugen, Book Editor

CUMBERLAND COUNTY LIBRARY
800 E. COMMERCE ST.
BRIDGETON, NJ 08302

GREENHAVEN PRESS

An imprint of Thomson Gale, a part of The Thomson Corporation

Detroit • New York • San Francisco • New Haven, Conn. • Waterville, Maine • London

THOMSON
™
GALE

Christine Nasso, *Publisher*
Elizabeth Des Chenes, *Managing Editor*

© 2006 Thomson Gale, a part of The Thomson Corporation.

Thomson and Star Logo are trademarks and Gale and Greenhaven Press are registered trademarks used herein under license.

For more information, contact:
Greenhaven Press
27500 Drake Rd.
Farmington Hills, MI 48331-3535
Or you can visit our Internet site at http://www.gale.com

ALL RIGHTS RESERVED
No part of this work covered by the copyright hereon may be reproduced or used in any form or by any means—graphic, electronic, or mechanical, including photocopying, recording, taping, Web distribution, or information storage retrieval systems—without the written permission of the publisher.

Articles in Greenhaven Press anthologies are often edited for length to meet page requirements. In addition, original titles of these works are changed to clearly present the main thesis and to explicitly indicate the author's opinion. Every effort is made to ensure that Greenhaven Press accurately reflects the original intent of the authors. Every effort has been made to trace the owners of copyrighted material.

Cover photograph reproduced by permission of Photos.com.

LIBRARY OF CONGRESS CATALOGING-IN-PUBLICATION DATA

Interracial relationships / David M. Haugen, book editor.
   p. cm. -- (At issue)
Includes bibliographical references and index.
ISBN-13: 978-0-7377-2390-8 (lib. : alk. paper)
ISBN-10: 0-7377-2390-4 (lib. : alk. paper)
ISBN-13: 978-0-7377-2391-5 (pbk. : alk. paper)
ISBN-10: 0-7377-2391-2 (pbk. : alk. paper)
 1. Interracial dating--United States--Juvenile literature. 2. Interracial marriage--United States--Juvenile literature. 3. United States--Race relations--Juvenile literature. I. Haugen, David M., 1969–
   HQ801.8.I68 2006
   306.84'6--dc22
                                        2006022929

Printed in the United States of America
10 9 8 7 6 5 4 3 2 1

Contents

Introduction

L ionel Kelly and Beatriz Chacon are students at Jefferson High School in Los Angeles. They are typical freshmen trying to make their way through their first year of high school. However, what complicates this journey is their relationship. Lionel is African American, and Beatriz is Hispanic. In May 2006, Erika Hayasaki reported on this couple in the *Los Angeles Times* and outlined the impact of being a teenager in an interracial relationship at Jefferson High.

Apart from the usual concerns of bullying and school work, Lionel and Beatriz attend a high school charged with a history of racial violence. As racial tensions within the community surrounding the high school grew, race-related violence erupted on campus in the spring of 2005. Many students were forced to choose sides along racial lines, and Hayasaki notes that these divisions remain a defining factor of social groups in the school. This segregation also contributes to the reactions that Lionel and Beatriz face from their peers. One African American girl disapprovingly refers to Lionel as "the boy that goes with that Mexican girl."

Outside of school, the teenagers experience a different set of circumstances. Their parents worry about the effects of the relationship on their school work. Lionel's mother sees Beatriz and her good study habits as a positive influence on her son. Beatriz's mother, on the other hand, worries that her daughter is too young to date and should be concentrating solely on school work. Both families live in integrated areas where Hispanics and African Americans live next door to each other. While some tension does exist between neighbors, generally friendly interaction prevails. Interracial marriages are not uncommon either. Lionel's uncles are married to Hispanic women, and he has biracial cousins. Although this acceptance does not provide solace for the teasing they suffer at school, it does offer hope for the young couple.

Unlike many who came before them, Lionel and Beatriz have the opportunity to continue their relationship, get married, and spend their lives together. While interracial couples do face trials, they are no longer kept apart by government laws that forbid them from marrying. Such laws were eradicated in 1967 when the Supreme Court found bans on interracial marriage to be unconstitutional. This ruling overturned a long history of antimiscegenation laws in the United States that began in the seventeenth century when settlers first came to the country. Since the overturn of these laws, interracial relationships and marriage have become much more common. The *Population Bulletin* reports that the number of interracial marriages in the country has risen from less than 1 percent in 1970 to over 5 percent in 2000. In addition to the growing numbers, recent polls suggest that there is also an increased acceptance. A 2003 Roper Reports study found that 83 percent of adults approved of interracial marriage as compared with only 70 percent in 1986.

These results show a positive change in the attitudes of adults; however, studies show that teenagers and young adults are even more open-minded. In June 2005 a Gallup Poll reported that 95 percent of eighteen- to twenty-nine-year-olds are accepting of blacks and whites dating. Within this age group as well, 60 percent of individuals surveyed reported that they have dated interracially. Kara Joyner, assistant professor of policy analysis and management at Cornell, also found that young people are more likely to be involved in an interracial relationship. She explains, "We think that's because relationships are more likely to be interracial the more recently they were formed, so younger people are more likely to have interracial relationships. This trend reflects the increasing acceptance of interracial relationships in today's society."

Some sociologists have sought other explanations for the higher numbers of interracial relationships among youth. Michael J. Rosenfeld, a professor at Stanford, and Byung-Soo Kim, a professor at the University of Missouri, cite increased geographic mobility coupled with greater independence of single, young adults as the main factors. Rosenfeld argues that prior generations of parents were able to exert greater control over their children, thus preventing interracial unions. Explained in this manner, the increase in interracial relationships is not necessarily the product of increased tolerance.

Most interracial couples can attest to the fact that, while they do not face the same intolerance that earlier couples faced, they are not always greeted with open arms. Many couples will recall that when they told their parents and other family members about their relationships, the announcement was not met with enthusiasm. Some were disowned; others were discouraged and told of the many problems that attend an interracial relationship, such as discrimination and the difficulties that any resulting mixed-race children would encounter.

Most interracial couples, however, do not need statistics or parental warnings to confirm that adversity still exists. They know that some people believe that interracial relationships are wrong and are not afraid to voice their opinions. While there may be comparatively few such ardent opponents, deep-seated racism pervades American society and can influence the reactions of even the most open-minded of individuals. Thus, interracial couples, like Lionel and Beatriz, have to contend not only with the trials of shaping a successful relationship but also with the pressures of an outside world that cannot yet ignore racial differences. Polls and surveys may suggest that the public is becoming more tolerant, but those in interracial relationships still have to work through racism, cultural affiliation, and identity issues to succeed. As Erika Hayasaki writes, "Lionel's dream is to buy a motorcycle and zoom to a place where violence and racism do not cloud his life." Until then, Lionel is content to hug Beatriz at school and anticipate a time when the two of them can go out to a movie together and do the everyday things that other couples do.

The authors featured in *At Issue: Interracial Relationships* examine varying aspects of the topic by analyzing social trends and offering personal opinions. Some of these writers address the many problems that interracial couples still face; others celebrate the collapse of old conventions and the power of love to triumph over all.

Interracial Relationships Are Becoming More Socially Acceptable

Francine Russo

Francine Russo writes about behavior, social issues, and the law for publications such as Time, *the* New York Times, *the* Atlantic Monthly, *the* Village Voice, *and* Redbook.

In 2001, between 5 and 6 percent of marriages in the United States were interracial. This marked a doubling of the percentage of mixed marriages in 1980. The growing trend in interracial marriage and dating indicates that society has become more tolerant of such relationships. While some people—especially those of older generations—are still uncomfortable with interracial coupling, America's youth are less resistant to what was once a social taboo. Part of the greater acceptance among young people has to do with the positive images of interracial relationships in media and advertising. These messages as well as the legacy of the civil rights movement have made younger generations more tolerant and approving of interracial relationships.

Tijuana Ricks and Michael Gillespie have been dating for three years and hope to marry. The African-American Ricks, 23, a Yale-drama grad student, and the Caucasian Gillespie, 29, a chiropractor, always loved the idea of blended-race children. But since Sept. 11, the idea of mixing up America's races has seemed even more urgent. "If we have

Francine Russo, "When Love is Mixing It Up: More Couples Are Finding Each Other Across Racial Lines—And Finding Acceptance," *Time*, Vol. 158, November 19, 2001. Copyright © 2001 Time, Inc. All rights reserved. Reprinted with permission.

more diverse children," Ricks urges, "they can educate others about different races and cultures and be more prepared for issues that might arise."

Brave words. But when it came time to tell her parents about Gillespie, Ricks hesitated, knowing his race would be an issue. "I told my mom I met this great guy who was smart and handsome and," she says with a giggle, "a little bit white." Her mother, she says, was "struck dumb." But soon her parents came to know and like her boyfriend.

If the couple marry, they will join a youth vanguard marrying interracially in increasing numbers and meeting greater—though far from total—tolerance from their families. The number of mixed-race marriages—between whites, blacks, Asians and Hispanics—has more than doubled since 1980, from 2.5% to 5% or, by some estimates, 6% today.

Peer group[s] and pop culture have long sent the message ... that interracial dating is cool.

In a new survey of biracial couples by the *Washington Post*, the Henry J. Kaiser Family Foundation and Harvard University, 72% of respondents said their families had accepted their union immediately. Acceptance, however, was lower among black-white couples, two-thirds of whom reported at least one set of parents objecting at first. There are still only 450,000 black-white marriages in the U.S., compared with 700,000 white-Asian and 2 million white-Hispanic.

Interracial coupling is actually rocketing up faster than the stats indicate, suggests University of Michigan sociologist David R. Harris. According to his research, 1 in 6 interracial unions is a cohabitation, so the prevalence of intimate partnerships among the races is greater than it appears. And casual dating between groups is even more common. The *Post* found that 4 of every 10 Americans said they had dated someone of another race and almost 3 in 10 said it had been a "serious" relationship.

Brita Roy, an Indian American, met her boyfriend George Jones, an African American, at Vanderbilt University, where the 21-year-olds are students. Although her parents in Michigan are immigrants from India and Jones attended all-black elementary and middle schools in Selma, Ala., the two say they have far more similarities than differences. They both attended small, upscale boarding schools; both are career minded. They share tastes for hip-hop music, Thai and Italian food, and shopping at Banana Republic. And they're well educated and affluent, like many interracial couples.

That Jones and Roy are a couple reflects partly the fact that their peer group and pop culture have long sent the message, whether through movies like *Save the Last Dance* or ad campaigns like Benetton's, that interracial dating is cool. "In adolescent life and culture, kids hang out together in all different kinds of groups. It's what's accepted, what one sees on TV, in the movies, in tons of advertising," says Ron Taffel, author of *The Second Family: How Adolescent Power Is Challenging the American Family*. "Now when kids date interracially, they're not doing it to rebel or upset their parents but because it's a part of life. It's a profound difference."

But if some experts see a change in the climate, it remains a change limited to certain corners of the country. Interracial couples are most prevalent in cities, university towns and large states with diverse populations: California, Texas, Florida and New York. And not all interracial dating is considered equal. Black-white couples lament that the historic divide between their races is still the hardest to overcome, whether dealing with their parents or their peers. At the Indian Springs school in Birmingham, Ala., recalls Jones, black kids felt it was O.K. to date an Indian, Korean or Latino, but they frowned on dating whites. Asian-white couples have it relatively easy, observes L.E. Hartmann-Ting, 32, a white grad student who lives in

Medford, Mass., with her husband Dr. Leon Ting, 30, a fellow in pulmonary medicine at Harvard. She feels curiosity rather than hostility from neighbors in her suburban apartment building about her Chinese-American husband.

In their hometown of New Haven, Conn., Ricks and Gillespie attract some "good-natured" comments. But they recall with a chill a road trip through Mississippi where they met with "scathing" stares when they held hands in a Wal-Mart. And while they and couples like them work on narrowing the divisions between groups in America, one couple at a time, their parents fret about their challenges. While Ricks' mother Loeida, a school librarian in LaPlace, La., gamely asserts, "My parents didn't choose for me, and I don't choose for my children," Ricks' father Thomas, a career military man, is less sanguine. "I'm a child of the '60s," he says, "and I remember segregation and the marches. Yes, things have changed, but not that much."

Interracial Marriage Is an Indicator of Racial Assimilation in America

Sharon M. Lee and Barry Edmonston

Sharon M. Lee is a professor of sociology and director of the Center for Health and Social Inequality Research, Department of Sociology, at Portland State University. Her research focuses on intermarriage, cultural diversity, and health-care disparities. Barry Edmonston is a professor in the School of Urban Studies and Planning and director of the Population Research Center at Portland State University. He has published widely on immigration, internal migration, and population distribution.

Intermarriage between blacks, whites, Hawaiians, Asians, and Hispanics is becoming commonplace in parts of America. This trend has been influenced by several factors, including increasing immigration, a narrowing of the socioeconomic gap between ethnic groups, and a growing social acceptance of interracial relationships. While the shift in public opinion has been slow and some opposition to intermarriage remains, the increasing number of multiracial and multiethnic families will continue to blur racial and ethnic divisions in the United States.

L ess than 35 years after the 1967 U.S. Supreme Court ruling that overturned antimiscegenation laws, racial intermarriage increased from less than 1 percent of married couples in 1970 to more than 5 percent in 2000. Hispanic intermarriage

Sharon M. Lee and Barry Edmonston, "New Marriages, New Families: U.S. Racial and Hispanic Intermarriage," *Population Bulletin*, vol. 60, 2005, p. 2. © 2005 by the Population Reference Bureau. Reproduced by permission.

increased from less than 1 percent of married couples to more than 3 percent in 2000. More telling, more than 10 percent of American Indian, Asian, Hawaiian, Hispanic, SOR [some other race], and multiple-race individuals were intermarried in 2000. Interracial and inter-Hispanic couples and their children live in every state and come from all socioeconomic groups. But intermarried couples and families are especially prevalent and are a growing proportion of the married-couple population in the West and Southwest, especially in states such as Hawaii, California, Texas, Oklahoma, and Alaska.

Increased intermarriage, particularly racial intermarriage, serves as a key indicator of two important social trends. First, as more people marry across racial groups, the social distance between racial groups is reduced. Second, racial intermarriage changes racial boundaries as family and kin, the most intimate of social groups, become increasingly interracial. In this process, the meaning and significance of race is altered.

Intermarriage Will Increase

Discussions and surveys about intermarriage in the United States used to focus on black/white marriages, yet most inter-marriages are between whites and nonblack minorities. While it is difficult to predict trends in social attitudes, demographic trends suggest that the increase in the number of Asians and Hispanics will fuel more intermarriage.

As more children from multiracial families grow up, they are especially likely to intermarry, adding to . . . the multiple-race population.

There are several reasons why intermarriage will continue to increase. First, as the Asian, Hispanic, and multiracial populations expand, more Americans will be living, going to school, working, and playing with people who come from racial and ethnic backgrounds that differ from their own. Increased contact, especially noncompetitive interactions among social equals at school and work will facilitate friendship, dating, and marriage between people of diverse racial backgrounds. By their very presence and growing numbers, multiracial Americans also demonstrate to the rest of society that racial intermarriage is a demographic and social reality.

Second, the U.S.-born share of the Asian and Hispanic American population will increase, and intermarriage rates are higher among U.S.-born Asians and Hispanics. U.S.-born Asians and Hispanics will be a driving force behind increased racial and Hispanic intermarriage.

Third, substantial numbers of children are growing up in interracial families. Although not all of these persons may report themselves as multiracial in censuses or surveys, our analysis of 2000 Census data showed that at least one-half of multiracial persons marry someone from another single race. Only American Indians have higher intermarriage rates. As more children from multiracial families grow up, they are especially likely to intermarry, adding to racial intermarriage and to the multiple-race population.

The Gap Is Narrowing

Fourth, the wide socioeconomic gap separating the majority white population from minority groups is narrowing, diminishing one of the major obstacles to racial intermarriage. Laws and efforts to help redress the socioeconomic inequalities perpetuated by discrimination have allowed growing numbers of minority people to advance. The improvements are especially large in education, an important avenue for social mobility in the United States. In 1960, 43 percent of whites but only 20 percent of blacks had a high school education or more, and 8 percent of whites versus 3 percent of blacks had graduated from college. By 2000, the gap had nearly disappeared for high school graduation, and it had narrowed for college: 26 percent of whites and 17 percent of blacks had graduated from college in 2000. Asians already had higher levels of educational attainment than whites: 44 percent were college graduates in 2000. Hispanics have lower educational attainment—in 2000, 11 percent had a college-level education or above. The narrowing of the education gap between whites and minorities and increased interracial contact at our nation's colleges and universities will also contribute to rising intermarriage rates.

Finally, the American public appears to be more accepting of racial intermarriage. Given American racial history and the tenacious controversies that surrounded race in American society, we should not expect rapid changes in attitudes about racial intermarriage, especially among whites. However, recent opinion surveys show greater acceptance of interracial romantic relationships, with majorities of respondents saying that they accept interracial dating and marriage. These shifts in public opinion are remarkable, considering that antimiscegenation laws were not overturned until 1967 and that, as recently as 1990, 67 percent of whites either opposed or strongly opposed a relative marrying a black person.

Countervailing Trends

While many factors point to continued increases in intermarriage, there are also countervailing trends that may slow or even reverse this trend. High levels of immigration will continually refresh the foreign-born population, and will affect future intermarriage rates for groups such as Asians and Hispanics (particularly Mexicans). While racial attitudes have shifted in recent years toward greater acceptance of intimate interracial relationships (as discussed above), there are still substantial pockets of strong opposition by whites to intermarriage between whites and blacks. In a 2000 survey, 38 percent of white Americans opposed their relative marrying a black person. While this is a dramatic decline from the 67 percent opposing such marriages in 1990, it is still a substantial percentage. Some members of minority groups also disapprove of intermarriage, with some viewing intermarriage as a form of racial disloyalty. Other observers have questioned the honesty of people surveyed; people may say they approve of interracial marriage because they consider it the socially acceptable answer. Apparent tolerance and acceptance of interracial relationships also appears to be contradicted by public behavior such as derogatory comments and looks of disapproval directed at interracial couples. . . .

Redefining Race and Ethnicity

Racial and Hispanic intermarriage produces new marriages and families that redefine the role and meaning of race and ethnicity in America. Intermarried couples, intermarried families, and multiracial and multiethnic children increasingly populate the American landscape. In some communities, especially in Hawaii and California, it would not be surprising if the average person were to conclude that intermarriage and multiracial and multiethnic children are the norm. Intermarried couples and families are racially and socioeconomically diverse, but most intermarriage still involves a white person married to a minority spouse. In this sense, intermarriage is "whitening" U.S. minority populations. As intermarriage continues to increase, further blurring racial and ethnic group boundaries, Americans' notions of race and ethnicity will surely change.

3

Teens and Young Adults Are Open-Minded About Interracial Relationships

Sharon Jayson

Sharon Jayson writes about family and social issues for USA Today.

Young people today are more tolerant of interracial relationships than were previous generations. Much of this acceptance can be traced to media images that positively portray race mixing. Another influential factor is the atmosphere of cultural diversity that pervades most schools and universities. Some observers of the trend, however, worry that racial color blindness may result in blissful ignorance of the social and economic disparities that still separate the races in America.

Ryan Knapick and Josh Baker have been best friends since fifth grade. Colette Gregory entered the picture in high school. She and Josh are dating now. Knapick is white, Gregory is black and Baker is half-Hispanic. To them, race doesn't matter.

"People are finding people with common interests and common perspectives and are putting race aside," says Knapick, 22, a May [2005] graduate of Indiana University who works at a machine shop and lives with his parents in Munster, Ind.

He and his friends are among an estimated 46.3 million Americans ages 14 to 24—the older segment of the most di-

Sharon Jayson, "New Generation Doesn't Blink at Interracial Relationships," *USA Today*, February 8, 2006. Copyright 2006, USA Today. Reproduced by permission.

verse generation in American society. (Most demographers say this "Millennial" generation began in the early 1980s, after Generation X.) These young people have friends of different races and also may date someone of another race.

This age group is more tolerant and open-minded than previous generations, according to an analysis of studies released by the ... Center for Information and Research on Civic Learning and Engagement, part of the University of Maryland's School of Public Policy. The center focuses on ages 15 to 25.

Another study by Teenage Research Unlimited in Northbrook, Ill., found six of 10 teens say their friends include members of diverse racial backgrounds.

A Generation Raised on Diversity

Unlike their parents and grandparents, today's teens and twentysomethings grew up with "diversity," "multicultural" and "inclusion" as buzzwords. Many were required to take college courses in cultural diversity. Now the media fuel this colorblindness as movies, TV and advertising portray interracial friendship and romance.

"Race is becoming less of a deal in dating," says Kriss Turner, a television writer and producer from Los Angeles who wrote the screenplay for the movie *Something New*, which opened [in February 2006]. The ensemble cast features Sanaa Lathan, Simon Baker, Alfre Woodard and Blair Underwood in a tale of a single black woman who finds her dreams of marrying an "ideal black man" shattered by her attraction to a white guy.

Some attitudinal changes are based in demographics. About 33% of those under 18 are racial or ethnic minorities, and about 20% of elementary- and high school-age students are immigrants or children of immigrants, according to the U.S. Census Bureau.

Racial diversity is especially common in college friendships because that age group is exposed to a wider range of people, and college students have more opportunities to become friends with peers of other races, says Anthony Lising Antonio, an associate professor of education at Stanford University, who has conducted research on friendship diversity.

It's not that young people are specifically seeking out friendships with other races, kids say.

"It goes beyond that to who you get along with," says Karina Anglada, 17, a high school senior in Chicago whose parents are from Puerto Rico.

Some experts say the notion of a generation that ignores race paints too rosy a picture.

The Pitfalls of Racial Colorblindness

Many would say a new generation that considers race irrelevant is something to be celebrated—the fulfillment of the Rev. Martin Luther King Jr.'s dream that his children "will one day live in a nation where they will not be judged by the color of their skin but by the content of their character."

But some experts say the notion of a generation that ignores race paints too rosy a picture.

They worry that decades devoted to ending racial segregation and creating a colorblind society may have created a new problem: a generation so unconcerned about race that it ignores disparities that still exist.

"People think this sort of colorblindness is a kind of progress, but I see it as more pernicious than that," says Tyrone Forman, an associate professor of African-American studies and sociology at the University of Illinois–Chicago.

His research, based on data from the University of Michigan's annual Monitoring the Future survey, suggests a troublesome side to racial colorblindness.

Even though young people report having friends of other races, Forman says, those friendships don't necessarily lead to a reduction in negative attitudes toward a racial group, because people view their own friends as an exception to whatever stereotype may exist.

Such feelings, along with studies that show less concern for racial issues among white high school seniors in 2003 compared with 30 years ago, makes him believe there should be more and not less talk about race, Forman says. . . .

"We have this sense that to talk about race is to be racist. That's what people have been told," says Forman, 35, who is black and is married to a white colleague at the university. "That's fundamentally what kids are reflecting back on us." . . .

It's more natural . . . to be attracted to people because of common interests and not because of common color.

Common Interests, Not Color

Where students go to school depends on where they live, which is dependent upon family wealth. [A January 2006] Harvard study found that segregation isn't simply a black/white divide but a multiracial one, in which whites remain the most isolated group and the least likely to attend multiracial schools. California schools are the nation's most segregated, the study found.

Gregory, 24, knows that firsthand. She was born in Gary, Ind., and grew up in Los Angeles; she was the only black person in a private school in her Bel Air neighborhood. She returned to Indiana for high school, the same Catholic school Knapick and Baker attended.

"It's more natural to me to be in a diverse setting and to be attracted to people because of common interests and not because of common color," says Gregory, who works in fundraising at a Chicago theater company. She earned two degrees from Northwestern University.

Baker, 23, who graduated from Loyola University in Chicago and is an accounts manager for a Chicago consulting firm, says his high school's diversity allowed him to be friends with whites, blacks and Hispanics. He says he's Hispanic, like his mother. His father is white but is unsure of his heritage because he was adopted, Baker says.

Knapick, who is seeking work in his college major of criminal justice, bonded with Baker playing basketball, running track and as Boy Scouts. Both are Eagle Scouts and earned their honors at the same ceremony.

Inevitable Mixing

Colorblindness might not always seem apparent early on; in high school, for example, students often sit at cafeteria tables largely segregated by race.

But several experts, including Pamela Perry, an assistant professor of community studies at the University of California–Santa Cruz, say such behavior is a phase. "In times of identity development, students clump with who they know and what's familiar," she says. "It seems to pass. Then they get out of high school and into college and they start mixing up more." . . .

A Gallup Poll on interracial dating in June [2005] found that 95% of 18- to 29-year-olds approve of blacks and whites dating. About 60% of that age group said they have dated someone of a different race.

Olivia Lin, 18, of Brooklyn, N.Y., is Asian; she's dating someone who is Puerto Rican and says her family is "pretty open to it." Lin, who will graduate in the spring [2006] with both a high school diploma and an associate's degree, in the fall will attend Brandeis University in Waltham, Mass., the only non-sectarian Jewish-sponsored college or university in the country.

High school freshman Aliya Whitaker, 14, of Montclair, N.J., says her mother is Jamaican and her father is African-

American. Her mother encourages her to make friends with those of other races.

"She's never told me to stick with my own people or choose sides," Whitaker says. "When my friends have *quinceaeras* (Hispanic girls' 15th-birthday celebrations) or bar mitzvahs (a Jewish coming-of-age ceremony for 13-year-olds), she encourages me to go.

"But she says: 'Remember where you come from.'"

4

Interracial Marriage in the Midst of Deep-Seated Racism

Tim Padgett et al.

Tim Padgett is the Miami and Latin bureau chief of Time *magazine.*

Interracial marriage is on the rise even in the American South where deeply held racist attitudes make such relationships especially difficult. A variety of factors have loosened the grip of tacit segregation and created opportunities for interaction between blacks and whites, leading to more interracial relationships. Acceptance of mixed-race families is increasing but some communities still react negatively, sometimes even violently, to interracial marriages.

To say Chip Edgeworth's father was unhappy about his son's marriage would be an understatement. Chip, who is white, says that when his dad learned he had fallen in love with a black co-worker named Yvette, the elder Edgeworth threw his son out of the house the family owned in Birmingham, Ala., and refused to speak to him. The reaction didn't surprise Chip. "I was raised so I couldn't stand the sight of black people," he confesses. "I was the biggest racist you ever saw." But then he met and fell in love with Yvette, a divorcee with three children. "She was the most beautiful woman I had ever seen," Chip recalls, "and she had a real intellectual spark

Tim Padgett et al., "Color-Blind Love: Once Considered Taboo, Interracial Marriages Are Now on the Rise—Even in Some Unexpected Places," *Time*, v. 161, May 12, 2003. Copyright © 2003 Time Inc. All rights reserved. Reproduced by permission.

to her." Yvette, for her part, was impressed by "what a remarkably generous person he was." After dating for a year, they got married in 1994.

The Numbers Are Growing Fast

Once a social taboo, love across the color line is becoming increasingly common. The number of interracial marriages in the U.S. has leaped almost 1,000% since 1967, when a landmark Supreme Court decision, *Loving v. Virginia*, voided state antimiscegenation laws that forbade unions between the races. Today there are more than 2 million interracial marriages, accounting for about 5% of all U.S. marriages, and almost half a million of them are between blacks and whites.

Yet even after the *Loving* decision, which required the state of Virginia to recognize the marriage between a white man and a black woman, Richard and Mildred Loving, the resistance to mixed nuptials in the South seemed to stay as firm as the reverence some there still have for the Confederate flag. It was only [in 2000] that Alabama became the last state to drop its (unenforceable) ban on mixed marriage, and it did so with just a 60%-to-40% vote by residents to make the change.

Of course, interracial intimacy has been a fact of life in the region since African slaves first arrived in the U.S.—and white slave owners like Thomas Jefferson began sneaking into the slave quarters at night. But what used to be branded clandestine lust has finally evolved into sanctioned love: black-white interracial marriages in Alabama have more than tripled, from 297 in 1990 to 1,000 in 2000, or about 2.5% of the married couples in the state. An additional 1% of Alabama marriages are unions also involving Asians, Latinos and Native Americans. "It's out of the bigots' hands," says Darryl Clark, a black mechanic in Birmingham who married a white woman 11 years ago. "It's gonna keep spreading."

Changing Demographics
Increase Interaction

Sociologists say the rise of an educated black middle class, the Sunbelt migration boom, "reverse migration" by blacks from the North and the fact that the U.S. military—most of whose bases are in the South—has become one of the country's most integrated institutions have increased opportunities for blacks and whites to interact as equals and develop romantic relationships. These factors combined to help join the Edgeworths. Yvette, 35, a claims auditor at the Social Security Administration in Birmingham, grew up on air bases in California and Germany before her family moved to Maxwell Air Force Base in Montgomery, Ala., in the 1980s, when she was a teenager. She and her first husband, who was white, had three children before divorcing in 1993. "In the military, everybody's pretty much one color these days," she says.

The lines, however, were more sharply drawn for Chip, 34, a machine operator who grew up in a largely segregated community in Birmingham. But spending time with Yvette and her family and friends opened his eyes. "I discovered the real world," he says. "They've got the same bills and problems I do." And although his father still won't talk to him, his mother accepted the marriage even before the couple's daughter Lauren, 7, was born. Still, there are awkward moments, even with the more welcoming in-laws. It's confusing "at Thanksgiving at my [maternal] grandparents' house, and my dad is the only white person there," says Chip's stepdaughter Ashley, 13. But, she adds, being part of a mixed-race family does have compensations: "I feel special because I can see the world through black and white eyes both."

Some experts believe marital integration will spawn broader social mixing between the races, giving more people that kind of dual vision. In Birmingham, say the Edgeworths, who live in a predominantly white, middle-class neighborhood, the once tacitly segregated public parks are slowly integrating as more mixed-raced families like theirs frequent them. "Multiracial living begets more multiracial living, period." says Randall Kennedy, a Harvard Law School professor and author of *Interracial Intimacies: Sex, Marriage, Identity and Adoption* (Pantheon). That's especially true, he adds, now that mixed marriage in the South is being accepted at all social levels— and working-class couples like the one played by Billy Bob Thornton and Halle Berry in the 2001 movie *Monster's Ball* have become more common. "That's the most potent development," says University of Alabama family-studies professor Nick Stinnett, "because it means a far wider portion of society now has a personal stake in doing away with the racial barriers that still exist here."

Young people . . . are even more color-blind than their elders when it comes to matters of the heart.

Some Communities Less Tolerant than Others

Melanie Clark, a white Wal-Mart employee who married Darryl, the black mechanic, in 1992, had previously been married to a white man who she says repeatedly hit her. After divorcing him, she explains, she was wary of hooking up with another hard-drinking, abusive "good ole boy." But Melanie, 38, was attracted to Darryl, 36, who showed a gentle interest in her, taking her dancing and teaching her how to hunt deer. Others were less pleased about their getting together. Some of their black neighbors in the rural community of Branchville, Ala.—particularly the women—were so angry about the marriage that they picketed the couple's home and openly insulted Melanie, calling her "white trash." Darryl, who admits to having had a temper back then, struck back when someone fired into their home in 1996, and a gunfight erupted. Melanie's son Adam, then 13, was wounded.

The family, including Melanie's four children and Darryl's daughter from a previous marriage, moved to more tolerant Birmingham soon after the shooting. But as stressful as that incident was, Melanie says it hurt even more when Darryl once asked her not to drive him to a job interview because he feared that his prospective boss, who was white, might object to his mixed marriage. As a result, she admits, she prefers that her 16-year-old daughter from her first marriage not date black boys.

Young people, however, having grown up with the racially inclusive ethos of hip-hop and who are comfortable meeting potential mates via the racially neutral Internet, are even more color-blind than their elders when it comes to matters of the heart. According to a nationwide poll in *USA Today*, 60% of U.S. teens have dated outside their race. Ali Zeidan, 22, a white Indiana native and computer major at the University of Alabama in Tuscaloosa, and Melody Twilley, 19, a black prelaw student, are among them. The couple became engaged this past Valentine's Day after meeting on the Internet [in 2002]. When they started living together, Melody's dad, a business-man in mostly black Wilcox County, "got mad and made me pay my share of the rent," says Melody. But then he got to know Ali. Now Melody says that instead of looking at her fi-ance as "a white boy out to steal our women," her father wel-comes him as a son-in-law-to-be with whom he can talk Democratic politics. He has also resumed subsidizing their rent.

Most marriages are, at one time or another, a struggle. There is little research to determine if interracial couples are more prone to divorce. But a University of Houston study [in 2003] found that these mixed unions are 30% more likely to have elevated levels of stress. A good way to avoid that, says Melanie, "is to make sure at the start you're getting married for the right, solid reasons" —and not, she adds, to make a social statement. Melody and Ali say they have considered the challenges they face and insist their marriage isn't just youthful idealism. "The bigger challenge for us is that I'm Catholic and he's Muslim," says Melody. "So we've thought this through."

5

The Entertainment Industry Is Still Shy About Depicting Interracial Relationships

Nicholas D. Kristof

Nicholas D. Kristof is a columnist for the New York Times. *He specializes in East Asian affairs and has written a number of books on the topic.*

Although interracial relationships are becoming more common in the United States, the movie industry has not chosen to reflect this trend. Film studios are too shy or too cowardly to portray interracial love in a serious light. Some are willing to show white men in love with black women, but this only hearkens back to power relationships between male slave owners and their female chattel. Hollywood has yet to break convincingly the social taboo of showing black men in loving relationships with white women.

One gauge of the progress we've made in American race relations in recent decades is the growing number of blacks and whites who have integrated their hearts and ended up marrying each other.

As of the 2000 census, 6 percent of married black men had a white wife, and 3 percent of married black women had a white husband—and the share is much higher among young couples. Huge majorities of both blacks and whites say they approve of interracial marriages, and the number of interracial marriages is doubling each decade. One survey found that 40 percent of Americans had dated someone of a different race.

Nicholas D. Kristof, "Blacks, Whites and Love," *New York Times*, April 24, 2005. Copyright © 2005 by the New York Times Company. Reproduced by permission.

But it's hard to argue that America is becoming more colorblind when we're still missing one benchmark: When will Hollywood dare release a major movie in which Denzel Washington and Reese Witherspoon fall passionately in love?

For all the gains in race relations, romance on the big screen between a black man and a white woman remains largely a taboo. Americans themselves may be falling in love with each other without regard to color, but the movie industry is still too craven to imitate life.

Or perhaps the studios are too busy pushing the limits on sex, nudity and violence to portray something really kinky, like colorblind love.

Hollywood's Lack of Progress

Back in 1967, *Guess Who's Coming to Dinner* helped chip away at taboos by showing a black man and white woman scandalizing their parents with their—chaste—love. In 2005 we have a new version of *Guess Who*, but it only underscores how little progress we've made.

The latest *Guess Who* is about a white man in love with a black woman, and that's a comfortable old archetype from days when slave owners inflicted themselves on slave women. Hollywood has portrayed romances between white men and (usually light-complexioned) black women, probably calculating that any good ol' boy seeing Billy Bob Thornton embracing Halle Berry in *Monster's Ball* is filled not with disgust but with envy.

From the beginning, the entertainment industry has lagged society in its racial mores.

Off screen, the change has been dizzying. At least 41 states at one time had laws banning interracial marriage. A 1958 poll found that 96 percent of whites disapproved of marriages between blacks and whites.

That same year, in North Carolina, two black boys, a 7-year-old named Fuzzy Simpson and a 9-year-old named Hanover Thompson, were arrested after a white girl kissed Hanover. The two boys were convicted of attempted rape. As Randall Kennedy notes in his book *Interracial Intimacies*, Fuzzy was sentenced to 12 years, and Hanover to 14 years. Pressure from President Dwight Eisenhower eventually secured the boys' release.

Then the mood began to change, and 1967 was the turning point. That was the year that the daughter of Dean Rusk, then secretary of state, married a black man. Secretary Rusk proudly walked his daughter down the aisle (after warning President Lyndon Johnson of the political risks), and *Time* magazine put the couple on its cover. That was also the year of *Guess Who's Coming to Dinner* and of a Supreme Court ruling striking down miscegenation laws.

Yet right from the beginning, the entertainment industry has lagged society in its racial mores. Films and television have always been squeamish about race: in 1957, on Alan Freed's ABC show, the black singer Frankie Lymon was seen dancing with a white woman. ABC promptly canceled the show.

Let's hope that Hollywood will finally dare to be as iconoclastic as its audiences.

There have been just a few mainstream movies with black men romancing white women, lower-profile films like *One Night Stand*. More typically, you get a film like *Hitch* where the studio pairs a black man with a Latina.

Dare to Mirror Reality

Popular entertainment shapes our culture as well as reflects it, and one breakthrough might come with the possible release of *Emma's War*. That's a movie that 20th Century Fox is considering, in which a white woman—Nicole Kidman is being discussed [for the role]—marries an African. It's great that Hollywood is close to catching up to Shakespeare's "Othello."

Let's hope that Hollywood will finally dare to be as iconoclastic as its audiences. It's been half a century since *Brown v. Board of Education* led to the integration of American schools, but the breakdown of the barriers of love will be a far more consequential and transformative kind of integration—not least because it's spontaneous and hormonal rather than imposed and legal.

6

Interracial Couples Must Deal With Public Attitudes About Race

Courtney E. Martin

Courtney E. Martin is a writer, educator, and filmmaker. Her written work has appeared in the Village Voice, Utne Reader, *and other publications. She is also an adjunct professor of Women's Studies at Hunter College in New York City.*

Being in an interracial relationship forces a person to inhabit two worlds. The intimate world of the relationship is typically color-blind, but the exterior world compels one to confront racism on a daily basis. Stares from passersby and spoken or unspoken judgments from others make those in interracial relationships continually aware that their being together is a political act. Even kind words from friends may secretly mask prejudices that sting. Negotiating between these private and public worlds can be mentally draining. Sometimes, though, it can be liberating to know that a loving relationship may help change social attitudes.

Being a white woman in a relationship with a black man is a schizophrenic experience. On the one hand, my relationship with my boyfriend is as personal and unique, nuanced and inimitable, as any human relationship rife with the complexity of love. When I wake up, tangled in a mess of his limbs and listening to his heavy breathing on a lazy Sunday

Courtney E. Martin, "Double Lives: Negotiating the Private and the Public in an Interracial Relationship," *Off Our Backs*, May–June 2004. Copyright 2004 Off Our Backs, Inc. Reproduced by permission.

morning, I do not notice that the chest that heaves up and down is black. Likewise, when we fight about his never-ending lateness or my propensity to grow unnecessarily anxious, our anger is colorless. When we make love, it is deep blue, not black and white.

But, when it comes time for us to leave our own personal universe and become part of the world around us, it is as if our transparent partnership is instantly colored in with shades burdened with meaning and legacy. Suddenly we must process the inevitable assumption by hostesses at restaurants and ticket takers at movie theaters that we are not together. We are forced to let go of one another's hands repeatedly as we walk down the street because in the quick, perhaps unconscious judgement, of our fellow New Yorkers we are two separate entities, fair game to weave in between. With the parallel stares I get in his neighborhood and he gets in mine, we are reminded over and over again that we are inherently politicized; even in the intimate gesture of a kiss goodbye or a hand on my back, we are bound into making a public statement. And perhaps worst of all, for me, I am propelled into a self-conscious state of doubt when one of the black women I know from school says, "Oh, you know how white women are: they go through their rebellious I-want-to-bring-a-black-boy home stage to save the world." The loaded look she gives me pierces me to the soul.

I strive to be proof to the world that human relationships can conquer culturally and politically prescribed boundaries.

Niceties That Mask Prejudice

The truth is that my boyfriend and I suffer very little when compared to any of the interracial couples that have had to exist within more conservative times and more conservative places. We have never been assaulted, ostracized or barred from going anywhere. We have never, in fact, been the targets of any overt racist discrimination. This I am endlessly thankful for. This kind of covert racism is more insidious and, therefore, sometimes harder to recognize and confront than more overt forms racism can take. In the past, when someone was not hiring you because you were black, at least they would tell you so instead of spending a lot of energy making you feel personally inadequate. American culture today is so mired in the paralysis of political correctness that I sometimes wonder if all this "respectful language" doesn't act as a slick cover-up for people's true prejudices. It is easy to avoid your own inner-demons if you never have to vocalize a straight-forward opinion. When my grandmother—with true Nebraskan farm girl roots—first saw a picture of my boyfriend she coalesced to the modern language so foreign for her tongue in order to deal with the situation without, of course, dealing with the situation: "Oh, African-Americans have such nice hair." Sometimes, when my boyfriend and I walk down the street we swear people walking past give us extra saccharine grins just to justify their own initial stares. The sweetness of it all is sickening.

In some ways, being in an interracial relationship today conjures the mental exhaustion of what W.E.B. DuBois called "double-consciousness" almost 100 years ago in his profound book *The Souls of Black Folks.* He wrote, "One ever feels his two-ness—an American, a Negro; two souls, two thoughts, two unreconciled strivings; two warring ideals in one dark body, whose dogged strength alone keeps it from being torn asunder." My boyfriend, undoubtedly, still experiences elements of this mental tearing-in-half on an individual level. I am amazed at his strength to experience it on a level with me as well. Similar to what DuBois so eloquently articulated, I feel at once part of a very personal, private relationship with my boyfriend, but simultaneously, I am a symbol of political and cultural deviance. I strive to be a good friend and lover to him, to laugh with him and inspire him and learn from him, but at the same time, I strive to be proof to the world that human relationships can conquer culturally and politically prescribed boundaries. I am at once a soul in love and a soul in storm.

We are ... lucky to have discovered a love that is both personally fulfilling and politically progressive.

Race Matters

Further muddling my ability to fuse my private and public sense of my relationship is the paradox of race in general. Of course race, this menacing and deadly ideology that America has paid lip-service to understanding for the last 300 years, is fictional. Of course there is absolutely no scientific evidence that race, as a category, exists. But on the other hand, there is also no denying that our preoccupation with this differentiation has been the driving force of our history. The most brutal and bold repression of individuals—i.e. slavery—has wrought sexual, physical, spiritual, and mental demolition. And that demolition lives on in its most insidious and damaging forms: the legacy of poor schools (not to mention job discrimination, housing shortages, inadequate health care and the prison tragedy). So while I would like to look some of our more determined starers in the eyes and shout, "Race is a farce! None of this matters!" I would be greatly mistaken. Of course, all of "this" matters. He is not black; he is Caribbean and Scottish. I am not white, I am Irish and Norwegian. And as we get farther and farther away, generationally, from our great-grandmothers and -grandfathers, even these categories feel increasingly irrelevant. Perhaps more importantly, he is not black; he is from Bedford Stuyvesant, Brooklyn. I am not white; I am from Colorado Springs, Colorado. But, and this is a giant, painful and crucial "but," the rest of the world sees us as black and white. We are locked into these categories by their perception and forced to play out the social and political ramifications regardless of how well-described we feel.

In terms of my public self, if I want to change American minds about the kind of connections that are possible between people of different categorizations, I must first convince them that race is a truly ridiculous conception, that what most of society, including just about everyone in my extended family, thinks is black is in fact Nigerian-American, Dominican-American, Caribbean-American etc., etc.; that what makes them comfortable—this over-arching and inaccurate concept of whiteness—is in fact thousands of forces: Italian-Americans and Jews and French-Americans and Zimbabwean-Americans. The more astute and descriptive categories that exist today are differentations, for example, by geography or by painfully relevant demographics like class.

The most empowering way to deal with the way my boyfriend and I are inherently politicized is, perhaps, to abandon our reluctant role as "interracial" activists and, instead, embrace the opportunity. We are, in fact, lucky to have discovered a love that is both personally fulfilling and politically progressive. While it is frustrating to know that our most casual public embraces are sometimes considered political statements, it also creates a space for true exercise of our ethics. We want the world to embrace a multiculturalism that exceeds the watered-down melting pot version so often lauded in popular culture. Our dedication to one another can be a small manifestation of the kind of cross-cultural connection that could truly change the world.

And after all this political and social commentary is said and done, the most important truth is that it is simply wonderful to be in love, no matter what the color.

7

A Black Woman's Reservations About Interracial Relationships

Shawn E. Rhea

Shawn E. Rhea is an award-winning journalist and creative writer. Her work has appeared in such periodicals as Color-Lines, Essence, *and* Black Enterprise.

People should be strong enough to love others freely without re-gard to race. However, this clearheaded thinking gets muddled when social stereotypes about interracial relationships interfere. It is also confounded when people of one's own race seem to be tempted irresistibly by the exotic lure of the "other" instead of by people of their own color. Often people fall into the trap of blaming those of another race for brazenly stealing away pro-spective mates. Such racist feelings are hard to shed, and some people have to struggle continually to maintain a tolerant per-spective—one that is accepting of both themselves and other people.

I have an affinity for black men, particularly artistic, cultur-ally aware brothas—poets, musicians and artists who sport dreadlocks or untamed afros. Since the late 1980s, my neigh-borhood of Ft. Green, Brooklyn has been the place to find them in abundance. It is not unusual to step into a cafe and see tables of black couples huddle together, looking as if they're sharing a wicked secret, or walking hand-in-hand as if

Shawn E. Rhea, "Black, White and Seeing Red All Over," *ColorLines*, Winter 2004. © 2004 ColorLines Magazine. Reproduced by permission.

they hold the strength of creation between their palms. But recently the neighborhood has signs of gentrification everywhere: from the new massive Pathmark grocery store to the rising rents to the white homeowners and tenants who are becoming regular faces at local haunts. As I turn the corner I am confronted with another sure-fire sign of urban gentrification; I see an interracial couple coming in my direction, holding hands.

The brotha is dreadlocked, brown and beautiful. The woman is attractive, shapely and sporting a geelee head wrap. I have seen black men with white women in my neighborhood so often recently that I no longer have to have that embarrassing internal conversation with myself: the one that says I am being racist, petty and insecure when I become upset over a brotha's choice to be with a white woman. I am struggling to be more accepting of each person's right to choose whom they love. I am trying to not take personally any brotha's decision to sleep with, date or marry a white woman, so I keep walking, and I force myself not to throw any glances that may be interpreted as disrespectful. But then, as we pass each other, the woman's eyes meet mine, and in hers I believe I see a look of defiance, boastfulness almost. The brotha shifts his head so that he can avoid our making eye contact. Suddenly I am angry. There are no words, no internal dialogue that can quell my feeling of betrayal.

Examining My Feelings

I do not want to be diagnosed with Angry Black Woman Syndrome, so I check and question myself. Is it my own fear of ending up alone, without a mate who truly appreciates and understands me? Is my own sense of worth and beauty threatened by the thought that black men who date white women have opted for a physicality that is impossible for me to realize, and, in doing so, have rejected me at my core, my very essence? Do I simply need something to blame for the fact that

I haven't been in a serious relationship for some years now? I vacillate between answering "yes" and "no" to each, check to see which response feels more like the truth and gets me closer to understanding. But I only find more questions. Now I ask, why are my ill feelings specific to black men with white women? I am not faced with the same uneasiness when I see brothas with Latinas, Asian, or East Indian women. Then again, the history between our people is different. My ancestors were systematically stolen and enslaved by white forefathers and foremothers—a legacy that, no matter how much we want to disregard it, is still reaping a stunted harvest. But I'm determined not to be a slave to this history, so I tell myself this hostility I have towards black men dating white women is irrational.

I am struggling to be more accepting of each person's right to choose whom they love.

The truth is, every important man in my life, from my father to my oldest brother to both of my deceased grandfathers, has devoted his life to building a strong, enduring, supportive relationship with the black woman who is or was his wife. I develop a list of affirmations for whenever I fall prey to the ugly, hurtful belief that black women have been abandoned. My invocations go something like this:

- I will not let someone else's choice define how I feel about myself.

- I will judge people based on their actions not their appearances.

- White women are not my enemy; oppression, racism, sexism and classism are.

- There are good brothas, kind brothas, culturally aware brothas, loving brothas in abundance, all around me everyday, who cherish and value black women, and could never imagine their lives without us by their sides.

Coveting the Other

My cousin Jamie is the closest thing I have to a sister, and she knows every secret about me that I would ever draw breath to repeat.

Jamie has her father's face and beautiful singing voice but got her straight, light-brown hair, fair skin and hazel-green eyes from her mother, who is white. When we were little, people never believed Jamie and I were related. "Are y'all jus' play cousins?" or "How come y'all don't look nothin' alike?" were the questions newly acquainted friends and even their parents felt compelled to ask us. As teenagers, Jamie was easygoing and popular while I was sharp-tongued and more aloof. New acquaintances, men in particular, always gravitated more readily towards Jamie. A large part of their attraction had to do with her personality; she is one of the most endearing people I have ever known. But there was another reason: an unspoken reason we didn't know how to name as children or teenagers. There was a high value placed on Jamie's long hair, fair skin and light eyes, and there were people who wanted to be close to her for no other reason. Still, there were others who disliked her for no other reason.

Being close to my cousin often gives me an uncomfortable view of racial dynamics that most folks only speak of in the abstract. But it would take years for me to realize that our friendship and kinship was the genesis of my internal battle against black folks' coveting of "the Other."

That realization comes one year when Jamie visits New York to celebrate New Year's. One evening during her stay we are visiting Charles [name has been changed], a man I've been dating. Tony, a mutual friend of ours, is also there. We are having a wonderful time listening to music and drinking wine when Charles starts teasing me about a guy who at a club the night before planted himself in a seat at our table when Charles went to the bathroom and all but refused to get up when he came back.

I remind him of another time. "Remember when we were at that club and that white woman came and stood in front of our table? She started dancing by herself and throwing kisses at you. She saw me sitting right there; she saw me looking at her like she was crazy, but she just kept on going."

We all laugh and shake our heads in disbelief. But I am not content to just compare notes with Charles about whose admirer was craziest. I begin making blanketed commentary about white women. "They are a trip," I continue. "Why are they so blatantly sleazy when they're going after men?"

I do not notice at first, but Jamie has become quiet. I go on to make some other less-than-complimentary remarks. When my cousin can no longer bear my comments she angrily snaps, "Shawn, stop dogging white women! You know, my mother just happens to be white."

My eyes fall upon her face, and despite her venomous tone I see only hurt. "Sorry," I say, knowing my apology is inadequate. I realize I have hurt my cousin in a way that I would not have intended at my angriest moment.

People need to be with the folks who make them happiest.

At home later, I remember an essay Lisa Jones, daughter of [poet] Amiri Baraka, wrote in *Bullet Proof Diva*, her book of personal and political essays on race and culture in America. Jones, whose mother is also white, tells of her own less-than-stellar feelings about brothas who pass over sistas in favor of white women. But she also writes that she fiercely loves her own white, Jewish mother, and that if one particular black man had not lain down with one particular white woman she herself would never have been born. I think long and hard on that statement, and I realize it rings true in the case of my own cousin and best friend—someone I could never imagine not having in my life.

Looking for Love

It is July 1999 and I am preparing to move to New Orleans. The unyielding pace and expense of New York City, coupled with a severe case of writer's block and restlessness are causing me to flee southward. While packing, I browse through some photos and I come across some of me on vacation with a former boyfriend. Usually these pictures fill me with a small sense of regret and longing, but this day it dawns on me that my fear of being perpetually single had subsided. Though I still want a partner, a husband, a man with whom to raise a family, I no longer wondered what I will do if this scenario does not become manifest. I know I will build a fulfilling existence. I find peace in this awareness.

I keep looking through the pictures and come across one of Jamie at her graduation dinner. She is tipsy, her eyes narrowed into small slits. It is a telltale trait of inebriation we both inherited from our fathers. I think about how often Jamie and I have visited each other in L.A. and New York, and I realize a chapter in my life is closing. I have grown at least a little. I rarely have a visceral reaction when I see black men with white women, and that is something for which I can thank my cousin. I am not sure when this particular union stopped feeling so threatening, but now I can actually say "people need to be with the folks who make them happiest," and not strain under the weight of my own politically correct assertion. I can truly believe it . . . most of the time. But I also know, even though I no longer feel like marriage is the ultimate prize, I want to be someplace where I can possibly meet a brotha with whom I can build a life.

As fate would have it, my first week in New Orleans I meet Franklin [name has been changed]. We are both writers, both new to the city, and we each have eclectic taste in music. Neither one of us is anxious to acknowledge an interest beyond friendship, however. He is a bit cautious, and I sense it is probably because there is someone in his life. My suspicions are confirmed when I meet his girlfriend, who is visiting from out of town. I am somewhat surprised to discover she is white, but I am relieved when my feelings do not linger past our initial introduction.

I am angry he has chosen a white woman instead of me, but I never speak this out loud.

Insecurity Revealed

Over the next few weeks Franklin and I meet for coffee, go to poetry readings, play pool, and take in movies. We talk late into the night, sharing our struggles to find our voices as writers. I tell him about the challenges of being a single, 30-something woman. He divulges that having made the choice to date a white woman there have been uneasy moments when people's judgments have intruded upon the sanctity and peace of their relationship; moments when he has felt the stress of their obvious cultural differences. But he says he long ago learned not to let other people's expectations dictate his choices.

Over drinks one night, it becomes obvious neither Franklin nor I really want to remain strictly platonic. "Long distance monogamy is just not very realistic," he tells me in a confessional tone.

"Yeah, I hear you, but I don't want to be the thing you do until the real thing gets here," I admit. What I don't say is that more than being concerned with whether I might be entering a relationship with a man who eventually will have to choose between me and another woman, I am concerned that this other woman is white.

I silently ask myself if he is dating a white woman because he has issues with black women or because he just happens to be attracted to this particular woman. But I feel it is impossible to respectfully ask a man with whom I ultimately wish to be intimate whether he has racial identity issues. I also am clear that few folks struggling with these identity issues are able or willing to give voice to that fact, so I bite my tongue.

Stereotypes hold power, and they have been bantered about so often people embrace them as truths.

I decide to observe his actions instead, reasoning they will provide a more accurate answer. Franklin and I begin dating and we agree to see where it takes us, but several weeks into our involvement he tells me the guilt of juggling two relationships is becoming overwhelming and complicated.

"I didn't expect to develop such strong feelings for you so quickly, and I can't let myself go there because I already have someone in my life."

I am disappointed and upset. While I shoulder much of the blame for getting involved with a man who is already in a relationship I can't help but feel betrayed. I am angry he has chosen a white woman instead of me, but I never speak this out loud. How can I reveal such an ugly, antiquated insecurity?

Motivated by Fear or Love?

Back when I was a child, "Brother Louie," a tune about an interracial love affair, was one of my favorite songs. I appreciated the defiant image it painted of two people refusing to let a societal taboo regulate their capacity to love, nurture and claim one another. I remember seeing hope in that powerfully subversive image. Why do I no longer embrace such feelings whenever I come across a black man who has chosen to break the taboo, I ask myself? I wish I could be that little girl again: the one who saw hope in the type of relationship I now struggle not to resent. But I cannot be her again. My feelings about black men dating white women are forever colored by the existence of a racial and sexual caste system that views black women as ball-breakers who are less-than-feminine, while white women are seen as accommodating and physically desirable.

I wisely know women, black or white, cannot be reduced to such derogatory stereotypes. But I also know these stereotypes hold power, and they have been bantered about so often people embrace them as truths. Some have used them as easy excuses for their complex choices, while others, like me, have felt rejected and sometimes find themselves questioning their own worth.

This epiphany strikes me at my core. Despite a healthy ego, part of my self-worth is inextricably linked to a desire to be loved, needed and cherished by black men. It is an innate want that I feel as strongly as instinct. But I am not an animal mating for the sole purpose of procreation. I am a woman—a black woman—who must separate the individual from the stereotype, the truth from the assumed, and I must find myself amid these contradictions. I must be willing to ask myself the hard question: by what am I motivated, fear or love?

I do not know if I will ever be totally free of this demon. I only know I wish to be free enough to love who I love, and secure enough to accept someone else's choice if they decide not to love me.

8

Many Blacks Continue to Oppose Interracial Relationships

Randall Kennedy

Randall Kennedy is a professor at Harvard Law School. He is the author of Race, Crime, and the Law *and* Interracial Intimacies: Sex, Marriage, Identity, and Adoption.

Although white America has traditionally been the focus of much of the outcry against interracial marriage, more recent criticism of black-white relationships has come from African Americans. Since the 1960s and the birth of the Black Power movement, some African Americans have argued that romantic relationships with whites weaken black culture and smack of disloyalty. These critics maintain that some black men's preference for white women, for example, reveals how white aesthetics are privileged in America while black aesthetics are degraded. This has engendered feelings among black women that they shall never measure up to white beauty and thus always be second-rate in the marriage market. Other critics fear that high-profile interracial relationships may convey to young blacks that obtaining a white spouse is the true measure of success and happiness. Not all African Americans, however, harbor such views. Several prominent black scholars have even argued that interracial relationships will help break down racial barriers and bring about more equitable integration. Regardless of these opinions, interracial rela-

Randall Kennedy, "Interracial Intimacy: White–Black Dating, Marriage, and Adoption Are on the Rise. This Development, However, Is Being Met with Resistance—More Vocally by Blacks than by Whites," *Atlantic Monthly*, vol. 290, December 2002. Reproduced by permission of the author.

tionships are on the rise in America, signaling greater racial tolerance among society as a whole.

Americans are already what racial purists have long feared: a people characterized by a great deal of racial admixture, or what many in the past referred to distastefully as "mongrelization." In pigmentation, width of noses, breadth of lips, texture of hair, and other telltale signs, the faces and bodies of millions of Americans bear witness to interracial sexual encounters. Some were joyful, passionate, loving affairs. Many were rapes. Others contained elements of both choice and coercion. These different kinds of interracial intimacy and sexual depredation all reached their peak in the United States during the age of slavery, and following the Civil War they decreased markedly. Since the end of the civil-rights revolution interracial dating, interracial sex, and interracial marriage have steadily increased, as has the number of children born of interracial unions. This development has prompted commentators to speak of the "creolization" or "browning" or "beiging" of America. . . .

The de-stigmatization in this country of interracial intimacy is profoundly encouraging. Against the tragic backdrop of American history, it is a sign that Frederick Douglass may have been right when he prophesied, even before the abolition of slavery, that eventually "the white and colored people of this country [can] be blended into a common nationality, and enjoy together . . . the inestimable blessings of life, liberty and the pursuit of happiness."

In recent years . . . couples in mixed marriages seem to be marrying younger than their pioneering predecessors.

The great but altogether predictable irony is that just as white opposition to white-black intimacy finally lessened, during the last third of the twentieth century, black opposition became vocal and aggressive. In college classrooms today, when discussions about the ethics of interracial dating and marriage arise, black students are frequently the ones most likely to voice disapproval.

Marital Integration

Despite some ongoing resistance (a subject to which I will return), the situation for people involved in interracial intimacy has never been better. For the most part, the law prohibits officials from taking race into account in licensing marriages, making child-custody decisions, and arranging adoptions. Moreover, the American public accepts interracial intimacy as it never has before. This trend will almost certainly continue; polling data and common observation indicate that young people tend to be more liberal on these matters than their elders.

In 1960 there were about 51,000 black-white married couples in the United States; in 1970 there were 65,000, in 1980 there were 121,000, in 1990 there were 213,000, and by 1998 the number had reached 330,000. In other words, in the past four decades black-white marriages increased more than sixfold. And black-white marriages are not only becoming more numerous. Previously, the new couples in mixed marriages tended to be older than other brides and grooms. They were frequently veterans of divorce, embarking on second or third marriages. In recent years, however, couples in mixed marriages seem to be marrying younger than their pioneering predecessors and seem more inclined to have children and to pursue all the other "normal" activities that married life offers. . . .

African-Americans largely fall into three camps with respect to white-black marriage. One camp, relatively small, openly champions it as a good. Its members argue that increasing rates of interracial marriage will decrease social segregation, encourage racial open-mindedness, enhance blacks' access to enriching social networks, elevate their status, and empower black women in their interactions with black men by subjecting the latter to greater competition in the marketplace for companionship.

A second camp sees interracial marriage merely as a choice that individuals should have the right to make. For example, while noting in *Race Matters* (1993) that "more and more white Americans are willing to interact sexually with black Americans on an equal basis," [educator and author] Cornel West maintains that he views this as "neither cause for celebration nor reason for lament." This is probably the predominant view among blacks. It allows a person simultaneously to oppose anti-miscegenation laws and to disclaim any desire to marry across racial lines. Many African-Americans are attracted to this position, because, among other things, it helps to refute a deeply annoying assumption on the part of many whites: that blacks would like nothing more than to be intimate with whites and even, if possible, to become white.

By the late 1960s ... increasing numbers of blacks felt emboldened to openly oppose mixed marriages.

A third camp opposes interracial marriage, on the grounds that it expresses racial disloyalty, suggests disapproval of fellow blacks, undermines black culture, weakens the African-American marriage market, and feeds racist mythologies, particularly the canard that blacks lack pride of race.

Talking Black, Sleeping White

Such opposition has always been a powerful undercurrent. When Walter White, the executive secretary of the NAACP [National Association for the Advancement of Colored People], divorced his black wife (the mother of their two children) and married a white woman from South Africa, in

1949, the *Norfolk* (Virginia) *Journal and Guide* spoke for many blacks when it asserted, "A prompt and official announcement that [White] will not return to his post . . . is in order." Part of the anger stemmed from apprehension that segregationists would seize upon White's marriage to substantiate the charge that what black male civil-rights activists were really after was sex with white women. Part stemmed from a widespread sense that perhaps White thought no black woman was good enough for him.

[Some perceive] that large numbers of African-American men believe not only that white women are relatively more desirable but that black women are positively unattractive.

By the late 1960s, with the repudiation of antimiscegenation and Jim Crow laws, increasing numbers of blacks felt emboldened to openly oppose mixed marriages. "We Shall Overcome" was giving way to "Black Power": improving the image of blacks in the minds of whites seemed less important than cultivating a deeper allegiance to racial solidarity. To blacks, interracial intimacy compromised that allegiance. The African-American social reformer George Wiley dedicated himself to struggles for racial justice as a leading figure in the Congress for Racial Equality (CORE) and the founder of the National Welfare Rights Organization. Yet many black activists denounced him for marrying and remaining married to a white woman. When he addressed a rally in Washington, D.C., on African Liberation Day in April of 1972, a group of black women heckled him by chanting, "Where's your white wife? Where's your white wife?" When he attempted to focus his remarks on the situation of black women, the hecklers merely took up a different chant: "Talking black and sleeping white." . . .

The "sleeping white" critique embarrassed a wide variety of people as distinctions between the personal and the political evaporated. At many colleges and universities black students ostracized other blacks who dated (much less married) whites. A black student who wanted to walk around "With a blonde draped on his arm" could certainly do so, a black student leader at the University of Washington told St. Clair Drake, a leading African-American sociologist. "All we say," the student continued, "is don't try to join the black studies association." Drake himself became the target of this critique. When he visited his old high school in 1968, he says, the Black Student Union refused to have anything to do with him, because he was involved in an interracial relationship. Drake's classmate Charles V. Hamilton, a co-author, with Stokely Carmichael, of *Black Power: The Politics of Liberation in America* (1967), was shunned for the same reason. . . .

Throughout the black-power era substantial numbers of African-Americans loudly condemned black participation in interracial relationships (especially with whites), deeming it to be racial betrayal. A reader named Joyce Blake searingly articulated this sentiment in a letter to the editor of the *Village Voice.*

> It really hurts and baffles me and many other black sisters to see our black brothers coming down the streets in their African garbs with a white woman on their arms. It is fast becoming a standard joke among the white girls that they can get our men still—African styles and all. . . .
>
> It certainly seems to many black sisters that the Movement is just another subterfuge to aid the Negro male in procuring a white woman. If this be so, then the black sisters don't need it, for surely we have suffered enough humiliation from both white and black men in America.

A Demographic Betrayal?

Although racial solidarity has been the principal reason for black opposition to intermarriage over the years, another reason is the perception that intermarriage by black men weakens black women in the marriage market. A reader named Lula Miles asserted this view in an August 1969 letter to the editor of *Ebony*. Responding to a white woman who had expressed bewilderment at black women's anger, Miles wrote, "Non-sister wonders why the sight of a black man with a white woman is revolting to a black woman ... The name of the game is competition: Non-sister, you are trespassing!"

African-American hostility to interracial intimacy [remains] widespread and influential.

Another letter writer, named Miraonda J. Stevens, reinforced this point: "In the near future there aren't going to be enough nice black men around for us [black women] to marry." This "market" critique of interracial marriage has a long history. In 1929 Palestine Wells, a black columnist for the Baltimore *Afro-American*, wrote,

I have a sneaking suspicion that national intermarriage will make it harder to get husbands. A girl has a hard time enough getting a husband, but methinks twill be worse. Think how awful it would be if all the ofay girls with a secret hankering for brown skin men, could openly compete with us.

Forty-five years later an *Ebony* reader named Katrina Williams echoed Wells. "The white man is marrying the white woman," she wrote. "The black man is marrying the white woman. Who's gonna marry me?"

Behind her anxious question resides more than demographics: there is also the perception that large numbers of African-American men believe not only that white women are relatively more desirable but that black women are positively unattractive. Again the pages of *Ebony* offer vivid testimony. A reader named Mary A. Dowdell wrote in 1969,

> Let's just lay all phony excuses aside and get down to the true nitty, nitty, NITTY-GRITTY and tell it like it really is. Black males hate black women just because they are black. The whole so-called Civil Rights Act was really this: "I want a white woman because she's white and I not only hate but don't want a black woman because she's black." . . . The whole world knows this.

Modern Hostility

Decades later African-American hostility to interracial intimacy remained widespread and influential. Three examples are revealing. The first is the movie *Jungle Fever* (1991), which portrays an interracial affair set in New York City in the early 1990s. The director, Spike Lee, made sure the relationship was unhappy. Flipper Purify is an ambitious, college-educated black architect who lives in Harlem with his black wife and their young daughter. Angie Tucci, a young white woman, works for Purify as a secretary. Educated only through high school, she lives in Bensonhurst, Brooklyn, with her father and brothers, all of whom are outspoken racists. One evening when Flipper and Angie stay late at his office, work is superseded by erotic longing tinged with racial curiosity. He has never been sexually intimate with a white woman, and she has never been sexually intimate with a black man. They close that gap in their experience, and then stupidly confide in indiscreet friends, who carelessly reveal their secret. Angie's father throws her out of the family home after viciously beating her for "f**king a black nigger." Flipper's wife, Drew, throws him out as well. Flipper and Angie move into an apartment together, but that arrangement falls apart rather quickly under the pressure of their own guilt and uncertainty and the strong disapproval they encounter among blacks and whites alike.

The second example is Lawrence Otis Graham's 1995 essay "I Never Dated a White Girl." Educated at Princeton University and Harvard Law School, Graham sought to explain why "black middle-class kids ... [who are] raised in integrated or mostly white neighborhoods, [and] told to befriend white neighbors, socialize and study with white classmates, join white social and professional organizations, and go to work for mostly white employers" are also told by their relatives, "Oh, and by the way, don't ever forget that you are black, and that you should never get so close to whites that you happen to fall in love with them." Graham did more than explain, however; he justified this advice in a candid polemic that might well have been titled "Why I Am Proud That I Never Dated a White Girl."

[With growing rates of intermarriage] black women feel [the] loss of potential mates acutely.

The third example is "Black Men, White Women: A Sister Relinquishes Her Anger," a 1993 essay by the novelist Bebe Moore Campbell. Describing a scene in which she and her girlfriends spied a handsome black celebrity escorting a white woman at a trendy Beverly Hills restaurant, Campbell wrote,

> In unison, we moaned, we groaned, we rolled our eyes heavenward. We gnashed our teeth in harmony and made ugly faces. We sang "Umph! Umph! Umph!" a cappella-style, then shook our heads as we lamented for the ten thousandth time the perfidy of black men and cursed trespassing white women who dared to "take our men." ... Before lunch was over I had a headache, indigestion, and probably elevated blood pressure.

Only a small percentage of black men marry interracially; one report, published in 1999, estimated that seven percent of married black men have non-black wives. But with poverty, imprisonment, sexual orientation, and other factors limiting the number of marriageable black men, a substantial number of black women feel this loss of potential mates acutely. In 1992 researchers found that for every three unmarried black women in their twenties there was only one unmarried black man with earnings above the poverty level. Given these realities, black women's disparagement of interracial marriage should come as no surprise. "In a drought," Campbell wrote, "even one drop of water is missed."

Disappearing Role Models

Compiling a roster of prominent blacks—Clarence Thomas, Henry Louis Gates Jr., Quincy Jones, Franklin A. Thomas, John Edgar Wideman—married to or otherwise romantically involved with whites, Graham voiced disappointment. When a prominent black role model "turns out to be married to a white mate," he wrote, "our children say, 'Well, if it's so good to be black, why do all my role models date and marry whites?'... As a child growing up in the 'black is beautiful' 1970s, I remember asking these questions."

[Orlando Patterson contends] that widespread intermarriage is necessary to the integration of blacks into American society.

Anticipating the objection that his views amount to "reverse racism," no less an evil than anti-black bigotry, Graham wrote that his aim was neither keeping the races separate nor assigning superiority to one over the other. Rather, he wanted to develop "solutions for the loss of black mentors and role models at a time when the black community is overrun with crime, drug use, a high dropout rate, and a sense that any black who hopes to find ... career success must necessarily disassociate himself from his people with the assistance of a white spouse." ...

The Powerful Influence of Interracial Marriage

Although Graham's view is widespread, there are blacks who not only tolerate but applaud increasing rates of interracial intimacy. The most outspoken and distinguished African-American proponent of free trade in the marital marketplace is the Harvard sociologist Orlando Patterson. Patterson makes three main claims. First, he maintains that interracial marriage typically gives people access to valuable new advice, know-how, and social networks. "When we marry," he writes in *Rituals of Blood: Consequences of Slavery in Two American Centuries*, "we engage in an exchange of social and cultural dowries potentially far more valuable than gold-rimmed china. The cultural capital exchanged in ethnic intermarriage is considerably greater than that within ethnic groups."

Patterson's second claim is that removing the informal racial boundaries within the marriage market would especially benefit black women—because large numbers of white men are and will increasingly become open to marrying black women, if given a chance. He notes that if only one in five nonblack men were to court black women, the pool of potential spouses available to those women would immediately double. According to Patterson, this would be good not only because it would make marriage more accessible to black women but also because larger numbers of white (and other) suitors might well fortify black women in their dealings with black men. As Patterson sees it, by forswearing nonblack suitors, many black women have senselessly put themselves at the mercy of black men, who have declined to be as accommodating as they might be in the face of greater competition.

Patterson's third claim is that widespread intermarriage is necessary to the integration of blacks into American society. He agrees with the writer Calvin Hernton that intermarriage is "the crucial test in determining when a people have completely won their way into the mainstream of any given society." In *Ordeals of Integration* he therefore urges blacks, particularly women, to renounce their objections to interracial intimacy. Higher rates of intermarriage "will complete the process of total integration as [blacks] become to other Americans not only full members of the political and moral community, but also people whom 'we' marry," he counsels. "When that happens, the goal of integration will have been fully achieved."

In the United States, openness to interracial marriage has been a good barometer of racial enlightenment.

A Barometer of Racial Enlightenment

Some may question whether higher rates of interracial marriage will do as much or signify as much as Patterson contends. The history of racially divided societies elsewhere suggests that it will not. Addressing "the uncertain legacy of miscegenation," Professor Anthony W. Marx, of Columbia University, writes that despite considerable race mixing in Brazil, and that country's formal repudiation of racism, Brazil nonetheless retains "an informal racial order that [discriminates] against 'blacks and browns.'" Contrary to optimistic projections, Brazil's multiracialism did not so much produce upward mobility for dark Brazilians as reinforce a myth of mobility. That myth has undergirded a pigmentocracy that continues to privilege whiteness. A similar outcome is possible in the United States. Various peoples of color—Latinos, Asian-Americans, Native Americans, and light-skinned African-Americans—could well intermarry with whites in increasingly large numbers and join with them in a de facto alliance against darker-skinned blacks, who might remain racial outcasts even in a more racially mixed society.

Historically, though, at least in the United States, openness to interracial marriage has been a good barometer of racial enlightenment in thought and practice. As a general rule, those persons most welcoming of interracial marriage (and other intimate interracial associations) are also those who have most determinedly embraced racial justice, a healthy respect for individualistic pluralism, and a belief in the essential oneness of humanity.

9

The Bible Does Not Prohibit Interracial Relationships

Nathan Carleton

When he wrote the following article, Nathan Carleton was a student at Duke University in North Carolina. There, he served as president of the Conservative Union and published several articles in campus and local newspapers.

The Christian God does not condemn interracial marriage. Although opponents may cite Bible passages that seem to support a separation of believers from other races, a careful examination of scripture reveals the flaws in such arguments. Commonly, the passages in question have more to do with restraints on relationships between Christians and nonbelievers and make no mention of race whatsoever. Other biblical references even seem to cast intermarriage in a favorable light. The most obvious conclusion that can be drawn from a thorough study of the Bible is that intermarriage is not sinful.

Anyone who has dated someone of another ethnicity knows that not everybody is fine with interracial relationships. Couples often receive awkward looks and stares in public, and many college students don't date outside of their ethnicity for fear of their families disapproving.

Polls show that a significant amount of Americans oppose interracial dating, even 40 years removed from the modern Civil Rights Movement. In 1987, fewer than half of Americans

Nathan Carleton, "The Bible and Interracial Marriage," *The Chronicle*, March 10, 2005. © 2005 The Chronicle. Reproduced by permission.

thought it was appropriate for whites and blacks to date. Today, the number is up, but only to 61 percent among Southern whites.

While some see these numbers as evidence that America is a nation of racist bigots, it's clear that not everyone who opposes interracial dating does so out of hatred for other ethnicities. Many Americans are in fact friends and neighbors with people of other races, yet are still uncomfortable with interracial relationships due to their religious beliefs.

Bible Passages in Question

"Interracial dating is sinful," some have said. "The Bible says two people can't be 'unequally yoked.'" Any Christian using the above argument needs to reread the part of the Bible he or she is referencing immediately. It has nothing to do with race, and it actually has little to do with romantic relationships.

The passage in question is 2 Corinthians 6:14–15. "Do not be yoked together with unbelievers," it says. "For what do righteousness and wickedness have in common . . . What does a believer have in common with an unbeliever?" The author's point here is not even cryptic: Christians should not join together as one with non-Christians. That's it. Whether this means believers cannot be best friends, close friends or friends at all with nonbelievers may be up for debate. What's not is whether the passage forbids interracial marriage or interracial dating. It clearly doesn't.

There is nothing sinful or wrong about interracial relationships.

Another passage that Christians sometimes cite during discussions about interracial dating is Deuteronomy 7. Here, God discusses marriage when instructing Israelites about living on the land he's promised them: "When the LORD your

God brings you into the land you are entering to possess and drives out before you many nations—the Hittites, Girgashites, Amorites, Canaanites, Perizzites, Hivites and Jebusites, seven nations larger and stronger than you—and when the LORD your God has delivered them over to you and you have defeated them, then you must destroy them totally. Make no treaty with them, and show them no mercy. Do not intermarry with them." Yes, in this scripture God tells Israelites to not marry people from other nations. He also tells them to "destroy them totally." Clearly, the issue here is not the color of the Girgashites', Jebusites' and Perizzites' skin, it's their culture. To argue that Deuteronomy 7 proves interracial marriage sinful is silly, as the situation is obviously a specific one, and the people's ethnicity is not the motivation.

Praise for Intermarriage

A far more relevant passage of the Bible dealing with interracial marriage is Numbers 12, where Miriam and Aaron are speaking bad words about Moses because of his marrying a "Cushite wife." That Moses' wife was a "Cushite" means she was from Ethiopia. It also means she likely had much darker skin than Moses, a scenario backed up by passages like Jeremiah 13:23.

In this story, God becomes very angry with Miriam and Aaron for criticizing Moses and his wife and even gives one of them leprosy. He offers not condemnation, but praise for Moses, calling him his "servant" and saying that "he is faithful in all my house." Were God opposed to interracial marriages, he certainly would have said something else here.

Other religions may have different things to say about interracial marriage, and hate groups opposed to it will surely keep trying to spin statistics and religious texts in their favor. But the bottom line is that the Christian stance on the issue is extremely clear. There is nothing sinful or wrong about interracial relationships, and anyone who says otherwise has either misinterpreted scripture or abused it.

10

Family Intolerance Is a Major Obstacle for Interracial Marriages

Maria P.P. Root

Maria P.P. Root is a clinical psychologist living in Seattle, Washington. She is a trainer, educator, and public speaker on the topics of multiracial families and multiracial identity. She is the author of Love's Revolution: Racial Intermarriage *and the editor of other books on race and diversity.*

Although interracial marriage has become more accepted in American society, hesitancy and resistance still exist within families of all races. Many parents are reluctant about their children marrying outside their race because they fear that the interracial couple—and any future children—will fall prey to harsh or perhaps dangerous bigotry. Other parents are more concerned with furthering the "purity" of their family heritage, in which religious and cultural affiliations are privileged. Sometimes an interracial union can overcome family opposition; other times it may deepen racial boundaries. Regardless, the prevalence of race mixing in the United States is forcing everyone to confront stereotypes and perhaps will engender new discussions about race and diversity.

Maria P.P. Root, "The Color of Love: The Tiger Woods Generation Is Far More Accepting of Racial Intermarriage. Is This a Gain for Tolerance and Openness or a Prologue to a New Backlash?" *American Prospect*, April 8, 2002, Copyright 2002 The American Prospect, Inc. All rights reserved. Reproduced with permission from The American Prospect, 11 Beacon Street, Suite 1120, Boston, MA 02108.

With at least three million people in the United States in interracial marriages, racially mixed marriage is no longer a rarity. And with one degree of separation—all the family members of these couples—it touches many millions more. Allowing a second degree of separation—friends, co-workers, acquaintances—intermarriage likely affects most people in this country. Younger people, on average, are far more open to intermarriage than those who grew up in an era of segregation. This trend is a major gain for tolerance and pluralism in America, and families that successfully navigate the challenge of interracial marriage often become more open generally. But large pockets of discrimination continue to exist.

Earlier in [the twentieth] century, segregationists expressed concern that civil rights would ultimately lead to greater acceptance of intermarriage. And in a sense, they were right. With more interracial contact has come less fear and more acceptance of the racial "other," and the ultimate form of acceptance is personal love and the marriage bond.

A 1997 Gallup poll found the highest approval rating of interracial marriage ever by both black (77 percent) and white (61 percent) Americans. The National Opinion Research Center (NORC) also has found increased acceptance. By 1994, when people were asked, "Would you favor a law against racial intermarriage?" 84.9 percent of 1,626 white Americans answered in the negative. Even more black Americans—96.8 percent of the 258 polled—also answered no.

Fear of Contamination

Nevertheless, interracial marriage can create deep conflict within families. Opposition reflects not just bigotry. It can reflect fears about loss of valued traditions, and concerns that children and grandchildren will suffer society's lingering prejudice. A NORC poll in 1990 asked Jews, blacks, Asians, and Hispanics how they would feel about a close relative marrying someone from outside their racial or ethnic group. Blacks were most strongly opposed, with 57.5 percent of 1,362 respondents against it; next came Asian Americans at 42.4 percent; then Hispanic Americans at 40.4 percent. Jews were the least opposed, at 16.3 percent, but also had the largest response neither favoring nor opposing intermarriage of a close relative (63.1 percent). Just over 46 percent of Asian Americans and Hispanic Americans were neutral on the question. These data show that despite the increasing acceptance of intermarriage in this country, people are not necessarily pleased when it becomes personal. Families remain highly protective of their most significant "product": future generations.

In their book *Multiracial Couples: Black and White Voices*, Paul C. Rosenblatt, Terry A. Karis, and Richard D. Powell suggest that disowning interracially married family members may be a way of disowning racially different in-laws. Through denouncement, families attempt to avoid possible contamination by an undesirable status or stigma. The NORC data and my own interviews indicate that people of all races sometimes fear contamination, though for different reasons. Whites may fear loss of privileged status for their children and grandchildren, while people of color may fear loss of cultural identity.

The hallmark of closed families is the rigidity of rules maintaining distance between "us" and "them."

If the couple has children, as most couples do, the children have a blood tie to both clans, which strengthens—and complicates—the links immeasurably. Parents who resisted the intermarriage of a child may soften their opposition when grandchildren come. Or their resentment may harden because of the embarrassment of a blood relation who is a mixed-race child. Late marriages (those that occur past child-bearing age) may receive less opposition for this reason.

Open and Closed Families

My attempts to answer the question "what differentiates those families who can welcome someone racially different from those families who cannot?" led me to think about families as open or closed systems of relationships. Open families most resemble an individualistic society in which interdependence is maintained and intermarriage is acceptable. Families that I term "pseudo-open" may encourage interracial or interethnic friendships and be fine with interracial dating, but they oppose interracial marriage. Other families are "pseudo-closed"; they are sometimes able to grow over time to greater acceptance of an interracial marriage—but this often takes years, and sometimes the birth or death of a family member. Closed systems typically correspond with monarchical family models, show less tolerance of individual deviation, and see race as a critical piece of the image or product and property of the family.

The hallmark of closed families is the rigidity of rules maintaining distance between "us" and "them." These families, while seemingly democratic in times of peace and harmony, tend to become monarchical in the disowning process, directing other family members' behavior toward the banished member. Communication moves in a single direction from the decision makers to the lower-ranking members—that is, from parents to children. The flow of communication may not change even when children are grown and well into their adult years. Cultural, ethnic, or religious traditions are often key parts of identity and help determine the boundaries that mark in-group and out-group status.

One immigrant group that has recently had great difficulty breaking closed ranks are adult children of South Asian families. Many were born or raised from an early age in the United States and are very Americanized. Intermarriage naturally emerges as a possibility for this generation, but their parents often insist that they marry someone culturally similar who has similar class standing. Some parents have hired private investigators to find out whether their children are having secret relationships; and some try to arrange marriages or place newspaper ads for suitable spouses for their children. They are often openly rude to girlfriends and boyfriends who are not of the "correct" racial, cultural, and class background.

Often the prospect of an interracial marriage . . . is seen as an act of blatant disloyalty, even as an act of war.

Marking and Perpetuating Racial Boundaries

Much of this rigidity stems from unchallenged prejudices or unrealistic expectations. In a culturally and racially diverse nation with tremendous, geographic mobility, educational opportunities away from home, and integrated workplaces, it is unrealistic not to consider the possibility that a son, daughter, grandson, granddaughter, niece, or nephew will fall in love with a member of an "out" group.

Until it comes to crossing the color line, closed families are not necessarily dysfunctional families which are unstable and chaotic, lack the capacity to nurture, and can be abusive. But they do tend to have certain rigidities, fears, and prejudices that are not easily changed by facts or experience. Their ability to act lovingly in the face of these feelings is limited or nonexistent. Interracial dating is explicitly forbidden. Closed families do not always engage in overt forms of racial discrimination, but they usually do their best to pass on a way of thinking that perpetuates the borders between the races, a way of thinking that forecloses critical thinking about race.

Disowning the Other

Often the prospect of an interracial marriage takes on mythical proportions and the partnership is seen as an act of blatant disloyalty, even as an act of war. Filial piety is assumed;

sons and daughters are indebted to their parents and must re-pay them for their sacrifices. Marrying the right partner is a filial obligation. The children of these families are caught in a horrible bind: sacrifice their own needs and desires or alienate their parents, perhaps permanently.

Closed families have narrow criteria for whom they will accept as one of the clan. They will open their ranks only to persons who guarantee betterment of the family position. Regardless of how a family becomes closed, the opportunities for growth and change are limited. In an extreme example of a closed family, Randall, an African American in his mid-forties, spoke about his ex-mother-in-law's inability to see him as a person.

> My daughter and my son are black and white. To make it brief, my wife called her mother in California one Christmas day and put our daughter on to talk to grandmother. She didn't say a word to our daughter and my wife gets back on the phone and her mother says, "What the hell is the matter with you? I don't want a nigger in my family!" And this is her grandchild!

Such behavior is not limited to parents and grandparents. Sometimes adult children disown their parents, as in the case of Linda, who married a white man years after being widowed by her Filipino husband. "My [Filipina] daughter really dis-owned me for several years," she said. "It is only this Christmas that we got a card. But in the card she didn't mention anything about having feelings against us or for us. She just sent the card to me."

One Avenue to Challenge Stereotypes

In his 1944 study of race relations, *An American Dilemma: The Negro Problem and Modern Democracy*, Swedish sociologist Gunnar Myrdal echoed W.E.B. DuBois's observation half a century earlier that the color line would be the problem of the twentieth century in the United States. Today, at the dawn of the twenty-first century, Jim Crow laws and other legal barriers are gone but not forgotten and we still struggle with race.

I doubt that intermarriage is the solution to all of America's race problems; nor is it necessary for all or even most Americans to intermarry. But it does provide one avenue for the challenging of stereotypes, particularly when it involves an extended kinship network of different-race and mixed-race kin. It is an opportunity to move into a different dialogue about race, a dialogue in which the voices of multiracial adult children and women and people of color can also be heard. And beyond its benefits to racial tolerance, interracial marriage demands democracy, openness, and tolerance within families.

11

Family Intolerance of Interracial Marriage Can Be Overcome

Yolanda E.S. Miller

Yolanda E.S. Miller lives in Hawaii. She and her husband are currently on staff at the First Presbyterian Church of Honolulu serving youth and young adults.

Family members and friends can often be the most resistant to a person choosing to marry across racial lines. Sometimes this opposition stems from fears that the interracial couple will suffer from racist attitudes prevalent in society. Patience and perseverance, however, can usually win over the skeptical and can prove to loved ones that the interracial union is a blessing and a sign of strength.

What people predicted would be a barrier in our marriage unified us.

Thanks to the era of political correctness, being part of an interracial couple no longer elicits blatant staring, but my husband Jim and I are still considered "unique." Still, I have been fortunate enough to experience very few instances of overt racial intolerance in my life. One of the first, however, occurred when I brought Jim home to meet my family.

I like to call God the Grand Director of my life because I see so many aspects of it reflected in movies. Like some of the women in *The Joy Luck Club*—a movie about the clash be-

Yolanda E.S. Miller, "Surviving Racial Storms," *Marriage Partnership*, vol. 18, Spring 2001. Reproduced by permission of the author.

tween two generations and two cultures—I am an Asian woman married to *lohfahn*, a derogatory colloquialism for a Caucasian, which translates roughly to "old rice."

When I brought Jim home, my younger sisters recognized him for what he was: a sweet, gentle, witty, and intelligent (not to mention cute) young man. Mom withheld judgment until she was able to observe his character and his decisions. My father was an almost-comical caricature of Steve Martin in *Father of the Bride*. He shook Jim's hand and grunted while looking away when they were introduced.

At dinner, he ignored Jim completely, speaking only in Chinese to my aunt (who, incidentally, was surprised to discover that he could even speak Chinese). A few days later, my mom suggested I rent the movie *Guess Who's Coming to Dinner*.

My father came to embrace Jim as the son he never had.

My Father's Fears

In later discussions with my father, I asked him why he disliked Jim. He quoted Old Testament commands forbidding the Israelites to intermarry with foreigners. I explained that I believed those laws were given to the Israelites to prevent them from leaving Yahweh for foreign gods due to pressures from a nonbelieving spouse. I briefly pointed out Old and New Testament teachings against racism, especially Galatians 3:28, but I realized that my dad was not interested in an exegetical debate. He was petrified with fear.

His fear had less to do with Jim and more to do with the racism he had experienced as a young Chinese man growing up in America in the 1950s. Most of the wounds were so traumatic that he could only allude to them and refused to discuss specifics with me. He was afraid that by marrying Jim I would be making myself vulnerable to the same kind of trauma.

Through many prayers, God's grace, the encouragement of my father's friends, and Jim's gentle perseverance, my father came to embrace Jim as the son he never had. But my father was not the lone naysayer. Others who counseled us cautioned us that our marriage might prove difficult (as if marriage itself was not difficult!). Some thought that the culture gap would be a troublesome hurdle to clear; however, I noted that the culture I had been born and raised in was as American as Jim's—it was our families and our ethnicities that were disparate. Some were afraid, like my father, that our future children would be targets of racism. A few even hinted that my actions were a renunciation of my cultural background. Although many of these concerns were raised out of a desire to care for us, I thought it sad that nobody thought to encourage us with the thought that our dissimilar ethnicities might actually be a help, not a hindrance, to us.

Our Marriage Is Stronger

Despite the overabundance of criticism and our imperfect love, God has made our marriage the instrument of his loving presence. He allowed the criticism, which could have debilitated us, to strengthen and unite our marriage. God led us to vocational ministries in a community that has a high percentage of "mixed marriages," yet where racial tensions remain high. I believe God has not only brought me and Jim together for each other, but to this environment together, to be an example of God's love at work beyond the barriers of skin color. I'm proud to be a couple that can serve in a way that many other couples could not.

The heartbreak of all those years produced more than just acceptance. It proved to me that I had found a man willing to fight for me. It proved that I was blessed with a love that could weather intimidating storms. It proved to me that I had a God whom I could trust to weave into my life a plethora of stories that would make life interesting and bring glory to the One who gave me life.

12

The Problem of Racial Identity for a Mixed-Race Child

Beverly Yuen Thompson

When the following article was written, Beverly Yuen Thompson was a graduate student at the New School University in New York City. She studies and writes about issues of race and gender.

Being a child of a white/nonwhite couple in America can pose challenges to one's sense of identity. Because the nation prizes whiteness, mixed-race children often try to reject their nonwhite heritage. But the desire to be simply defined as a person, not a mixed-race person, is always frustrated by media images and social attitudes that subtly or overtly draw attention to the disparity between being white and being other. Hopefully, over time, one learns to confront the stereotypes and deflate attitudes of racial superiority. By investigating both sides of his or her heritage, a mixed-race person can experience personal growth and, by accepting the unique character of a mixed-race life, discover that many people in America share a similar background.

My parents tell me that at age two and a half, I ran around the house shouting "I'm an American, I'll speak English!" I rejected my mother's heritage in vicious outbursts as she told me bedtime stories about "long loy lew" and used picture flash cards with words on them I could only pro-

Beverly Yuen Thompson, "Memories from a Mixed Race Childhood," *Iris: A Journal About Women*, Spring 2002. Reproduced by permission of the author.

nounce haltingly. I had no desire to learn a language that would set me apart from my school peers. Without speaking Chinese, my whiteness would have more validity. My mother doesn't appear ashamed when she reminds me of the story—instead she smiles and teases me in a good-natured way. My father tisks, "It's a shame you didn't learn Chinese." His face is not illuminated with pride by his "daddy's girl," the daughter who desired to become him, a white American. In those moments, I want him to explain the mystery to me: How did I learn at two-and-a-half that to speak anything other than English would make me less than "American"?

Even with my narrow views on language as a child, I always secretly delighted in my mother's linguistic ability during our trips to Seattle, where we could eat in Chinatown, despite my father's grumbling resistance. At those moments I would soak up all the names of the dim sum dishes and ask the waiter for "my daan" to my mother's beaming delight. The waiters always looked at me, turned to my mother, and asked, "Can she speak Chinese?" Shaking her head, the waiters would chastise her deficiencies in motherhood. During these moments, the potential of a bilingual existence would send a thrill of excitement through me: Oh the doors that it would open. Upon return to Spokane, these thoughts faded; there were few bilingual people in my hometown to remind me of this distant desire.

Unfamiliar Territory

Only in Seattle's Chinatown could my mother culturally relax, surrounded by her native cuisine and language. On these trips there was not any negotiation, compromise or discussion about food selection. Her taste buds came back to life after the months, years, of consuming Americanized Chinese food on the Spokane boulevards where the only Chinese people present were the owners. She would stock up on Chinese cooking supplies, pulling me behind her through the maze of cluttered store isles, arguing in loud, colorful Chinese, like someone preparing for a drought. My father would follow along in defeat, protesting against the women leading him around in unfamiliar territory. He verbalized his longing for his comfort food, his safe ground. He wanted to eat at McDonald's "You can eat at McDonald's anywhere. How often do I get to have yum cha?" Indeed, this was perhaps the only place in the entire state of Washington where one could savor the delicious dim sum.

Perhaps if I had learned Chinese, my father's patriarchy within our home would have been undermined.

But my father understood the important role of food in cultural imperialism, even in the microcosm of our family. Rarely did my mother cook Chinese food in our home, but rather, she cooked his favorite dishes. When she would place steaming noodle soup in front of him with a ceramic Chinese spoon sticking out of the bowl, he would jump up and throw the spoon in the sink, walk over to the cabinet, pull out a thin metal spoon and chastise her, "I want my Army general spoon with the stripes, not that clunker."

Occasionally, my aunt would stop by with her children and fill the house with loud guttural Chinese that would scare my father off to the basement. I was impressed that my younger cousins could understand what our mothers were discussing, yet they also rejected the language and would only reply in English. My aunt was much more insistent with them. She would continue in Chinese; they would retort with English. My mother would slowly recount the conversation between herself and her sister after my aunt had left the house. My father would become enraged and shout out, "I'm going to impose a new rule: Only English spoken in this household! Your sister can tell me what she thinks to my face in English, not in her secret Chinese."

Perhaps if I had learned Chinese, my father's patriarchy within our home would have been undermined—something he would not tolerate. I imagine the power shift that would have come from my mother and me having our own secret language. My father can pity the lost opportunity, but had it not been lost, it certainly would have created tension.

My parents rarely spent time analyzing their own racial situation.

Parental Unconcern

The truth is, my parents rarely spent time analyzing their own racial situation. When I asked my father to be interviewed by a journalist on cross-racial relationships, he didn't know what to say except, "Well, I've never thought about your mother and me that way. I wouldn't know what to say." He never thought deeply about his racial privilege and the consequent effects on his life. Occasionally, he would admit that, because of her nonwhite ethnicity, my mother had it rough applying for jobs in Spokane. Yet he would never admit that he had it easy because of his race and gender. The doors to professional accomplishment were thrown wide open to him. My mother's race denied her entry into many professions where she could have succeeded. Even as my father was lulled into racial unconsciousness by the glare of his white skin, my mother's struggle was a shocking counterpoint to his theories of level playing fields. Accustomed to blaming the victim for not trying hard enough and not succeeding, he had to admit that something was awry—my mother tried harder than anyone did.

I started wondering what race I was when I had to fill out the ethnicity question on the school forms. I asked my father about this dilemma and he raised his eyebrows in hesitation and answered, "I don't know, I guess you could put one or the other." Indeed, "one or the other" was the answer that the form attempted to draw forth. But which one? Which one? How could I choose between identifying with my mother over my father, my father over my mother? I asked my mother for a solution. She would smile absently and respond, "Why, you are Amerasian." Yet Amerasian was not an option on the simplistic forms that categorize people into artificial boxes. My parents never defined me racially. They never gave me a ready made, self-descriptive term that I could wear like a badge.

White men use my race as a sexual pick-up; they attempt to . . . scrutinize my level of exoticness.

Experiences with Racism

So, I was ill-prepared when I was sixteen and attended summer school in Seattle, along with one hundred international students from Asia and four American white girls. It was the first time that I was around Asians almost exclusively, and I felt extremely isolated. I was terrified that they would all speak the same language and I would be left mute. The white girls looked at me as if I was a foreigner. They commented with surprise on my knowledge of baseball during an outing at a Mariners game—I had been explaining the rules to my Chinese comrades. It was the first time the white girls reconsidered their notion of me as they thought, How does she know so much about baseball? It was also the first time they talked to me. Once they realized that I was from Washington State just like them, and only spoke English, they became more sociable. But I had been confused by their reaction: Baseball had been my passion, how could the white girls make such a mistake?

When racist things happened to me outside my home, I rarely told my father who couldn't understand. Like the time when I ran into an old white woman in an elevator at the hospital and she asked, "Where are you from?" My father merely chuckled and said, "Little did she know you were born in that building. She thought you were from China!" Or the time when I was helping a visiting professor from China find housing. I spoke on the phone with the white woman who was renting the room, and explained that I was a student assisting a visiting professor. The white woman fetishized all things Chinese—she had been to China and loved it, and she loved to see how truly different those Chinese people were. When Ji Min and I arrived at the woman's door, she threw it open and exclaimed with frustration, "Well, which one of you is from China!" She spoke with such a sense of entitlement, as if she were offended by such trickery.

Not Some Sweet Little Asian Girl

Often these encounters with racism were, and still are, completely intertwined with gender and sexuality. White men use my race as a sexual pick-up; they attempt to pry me open and scrutinize my level of exoticness. They feel entitled to enter my space, rest a hand on my skin, and ask personal questions about my identity. All of these incidents have added up and contribute to my stockpile of ready-made verbal comebacks. It leaves me entering the world with a strong shield of defensiveness. Constantly, I am put on guard as I protect myself from all the jeers, racial comments, stereotypes, and jokes. "Is your name Me Ling?" "Oh, konitchiwa, you speak English?" "Where you from? No, I mean, where are you really from—like, where are your parents from?" "You know—what are you?" Over the last few years I have shot back angry retorts, no longer willing to be patient with racists as they attempt to pigeonhole me. If they are allowed to ask my race, I am allowed to answer in any way I choose, including with silence or anger. Why are they compelled to question my race in order to relate to me?

I am no longer willing to hide, nor to ignore or forget these comments. The questioner is often utterly shocked that I should be offended. After all, they were just curious, they didn't mean anything, they really think it's cool, and so on. Yet these questions stem from a deep-rooted obsession with race, fueled by racism and white supremacy. We cannot ignore the history of this country, and how that shapes every racial encounter. Not only are they shocked that I should be offended by their racial inquisition, but it counters their stereotyped expectations. They think I'll giggle at their question, or be flattered at the racial attention from a white man. When I respond with curt anger and disapproval to their questions, they are utterly flabbergasted. I'm not some sweet little Asian girl after all.

Writing about my mixed race identity has contributed a great deal to my personal growth.

Understanding History

I initiated a serious study of mixed race issues while attending graduate school. Being in a Women's Studies program, I was encouraged to explore many aspects of identity. It was the first time I discovered books on this topic, and I was inspired. I joined mixed race groups and attended conferences in which I was among hundreds of people like me. My story was similar to so many—and this was quite a comfort. I met people who had also rejected their mother's native language, who faltered over the racial question on forms, even those with familial tensions like mine. And I met people who celebrated their dual heritage, who learned about all their cultures, and who were proud of their identity. It was the first time I began to write about myself, with a voice rooted in identity.

I realized that no matter how much I rejected my ethnic background, it would nonetheless mark my existence within this country. I learned a great deal about U.S. history from the perspective of Asian American struggles and inter-racial contact over the last hundred years. For example, the Supreme Court decision that ended anti-miscegenation laws occurred ten years previous to my parents' marriage. Just ten years earlier and their marriage may have been illegal! My father was largely shaped by the national events that transpired since his birth in 1926—events that created his perspectives on race and nationalism. During WWII he sat in a graduate class in the Midwest and was surprised that his Japanese teacher wasn't interned. Such historical events crafted perspectives he holds to this day.

No matter how much I rejected my ethnic background, it would nonetheless mark my existence within this country.

Writing about my mixed race identity has contributed a great deal to my personal growth. I am grounded in a firm knowledge of my history and am no longer ashamed of my ethnic background. Now I realize the asset of speaking Chinese. Having moved to New York City I live in Chinatown—in the same apartment where my mother lived when she first came to the United States thirty years earlier.

Cantonese surrounds me as I walk down the street in my neighborhood, and I can recognize the few words that my mother taught me. Yet when the waiters speak to me in Chinese, I respond in English. If my mother were there, they would turn to her and ask, "Can she speak Chinese?" My mother would be compelled to shake her head and receive another lecture in her deficiencies. Yet the distant familiarity of the language surprises me, and perhaps it is never too late. Just last week I called my mom on the telephone to ask for a few more words to learn. I teased her that she'd be surprised to know I've passed for Chinese three times already, by responding in Cantonese to my neighbors in the building.

Organizations to Contact

The editors have compiled the following list of organizations concerned with the issues debated in this book. The descriptions are derived from materials provided by the organizations. All have publications or information available for interested readers. The list was compiled on the date of the publication of the present volume; the information provided here may change. Be aware that many organizations take several weeks or longer to respond to inquiries, so allow as much time as possible.

American Civil Liberties Union (ACLU)
125 Broad St., 18⁰ Floor, New York, NY   10004-2400
(212) 549-2500
e-mail: aclu@aclu.org
Web site: www.aclu.org

The ACLU is a national organization that works to defend Americans' civil rights as guaranteed by the U.S. Constitution. It provides legal defense, research and education. The ACLU publishes and distributes policy statements, pamphlets and an online newsletter available for e-mail subscription.

Intermix
PO Box 29441, London   NW1 8FZ
   England
0207-485-2869
e-mail: contact@intermix.org.uk
Web site: www.intermix.org.uk

Intermix is an organization based in the United Kingdom with the goal of uniting people of all races and promoting increased racial understanding. Intermix is a nonprofit organization that focuses mainly on providing information about mixed-race individuals and families. It offers an extensive database of varying media on the topic of mixed-race individuals and publishes a monthly newsletter.

Interracial Voice (IV)

PO Box 560185, College Point, NY   11356-0185

(718) 909-1878

e-mail: intvoice@webcom.com

Web site: www.webcom.com/~intvoice

IV is a group that provides information about multiracial issues and offers individuals an opportunity to voice their opinions about these topics. The organization's Web site contains many links to multiracial resources including other sites, news articles, and census information.

MAVIN Foundation

600 First Ave., Suite 600, Seattle, WA   98104

(206) 622-7101 • fax: (206) 622-2231

e-mail: info@mavinfoundation.org

Web site: www.mavinfoundation.org

The MAVIN Foundation is a cultural identity support group that encourages individuals to connect with their racial and ethnic background. The ultimate goal is to redefine the culture of racial and ethnic heritage in the United States and reject old notions of race. The organization publishes the magazine *MAVIN* and other books, pamphlets, and educational materials. It also offers a student internship program.

Multicultural Council of Saskatchewan (MCoS)

369 Part St., Regina   SK S4N 5B2

   Canada

(306) 721-2767 • fax: (306) 721-3342

e-mail: mcos@accesscomm.ca

Web site: http://mcos.sask.com

MCoS promotes positive cross-cultural relations and the recognition of cultural diversity. Its publications include *Faces Magazine* and *Multiculturalism Matters*. MCoS also distributes information concerning multiculturalism, such as multifaith calendars, to the public.

Multiethnic Education Program (ME Program)

1581 LeRoy Ave, Berkeley, CA   94708
(510) 644-1000 • fax: (510) 525-4106
Web site: www.multiethniceducation.org

The ME Program promotes new attitudes toward multiethnic education for children. It offers training and educational resources for individuals involved in education and childcare fields as well as for students. The program publishes the multimedia training guides such as *Serving Biracial and Multiethnic Children and Their Families* and *My People Are . . . Youth Pride in Mixed Heritage.*

National Urban League

120 Wall St., New York, NY   10005
(212) 558-5600 • fax: (212) 344-5332
e-mail: info@nul.org
Web site www.nul.org

A community service agency, the National Urban League aims to eliminate institutional racism in the United States. It also provides services for minorities who experience discrimination in employment, housing, welfare, and other areas. It publishes numerous journals and studies on diversity issues and the black American experience.

New Demographic

244 Fifth Ave, Suite J230, New York, NY   10001-7604
(917) 291-5227
e-mail: team@newdemographic.com
Web site: www.newdemographic.com

New Demographic is a diversity training firm codirected by Jen Chau and Carmen Van Kerckhove. In addition to workshops that offer new perspectives on multiracial topics, the organization publishes a monthly newsletter available on its Web site. New Demographic also cohosts the biweekly podcast radio show *Addicted to Race* about race in America and coedits *Mixed Media Watch,* an online Web log that provides posts on representations of multiracial families and individuals in the media.

Project RACE
PO Box 2366, Los Banos, CA   93635
fax: (209) 826-2510
e-mail: projrac@aol.com
Web site: www.projectrace.com

Project RACE is an advocacy group that promotes new methods for racial classification on all forms that request racial data. One branch of the group is Teen Project RACE, which allows teenagers to have a voice in multiracial issues.

Sojourners
3333 Fourteenth St. NW, Suite 200, Washington, DC   20010
(202) 328-8842 • fax: (202) 328-8757
e-mail: sojourners@sojo.net
Web site: www.sojourners.com

Sojourners is an ecumenical Christian organization committed to racial justice and reconciliation between races. It publishes *America's Original Sin* as well as the monthly *Sojourners* magazine.

Tolerance.org
c/o The Southern Poverty Law Center
Montgomery, AL   36104
(334) 956-8200 • fax: (334) 956-8488
Web site: www.tolerance.org

Tolerance.org is an online group that provides information about increasing diversity and breaking down hate and racial barriers. It provides both online resources and print materials for children, teens, parents, and educators. There is a bimonthly newsletter available for online subscription and free classroom resources for teachers. The group receives support from the Southern Poverty Law Center.

United States Commission on Civil Rights
624 Ninth St. NW, Washington, DC   20425
(202) 376-7700
Web site: www.usccr.gov

A fact-finding body, the United States Commission on Civil Rights reports directly to Congress and the president on the effectiveness of equal opportunity programs and laws. A catalog of its numerous publications can be obtained from its Web site.

Bibliography

Books

Erica Chito Childs	*Navigating Interracial Borders: Black-White Couples and Their Social Worlds.* New Brunswick, NJ: Rutgers University Press, 2005.
Joel Crohn	*Mixed Matches: How to Create Successful Interracial, Interethnic and Interfaith Relationships.* New York: Ballantine, 1995.
Heather M. Dalmage	*Tripping on the Color Line: Black-White Multiracial Families in a Racially Divided World.* New Brunswick, NJ: Rutgers University Press, 2000.
Peggy Gillespie	*Of Many Colors: Portraits of Multiracial Families.* Amherst, MA: University of Amherst Press, 1997.
Martha Hodes, ed.	*Sex, Love, Race: Crossing Boundaries in North American History.* New York: New York University Press, 1999.
John Johnson	*It Ain't All Good: Why Black Men Should Not Date White Women.* Chicago: African American Images, 2004.
Randall Kennedy	*Interracial Intimacies: Sex, Marriage, Identity and Adoption.* New York: Pantheon, 2003.
Elliott Lewis	*My Journeys in Multiracial America.* New York: Carroll and Graf, 2006.

Alex Lubin — *Romance and Rights: The Politics of Interracial Intimacy, 1945–1954.* Jackson: University of Mississippi, 2005.

Robert P. McNamara, Maria Tempenis, and Beth Walton — *Crossing the Line.* Westport, CT: Greenwood, 1999.

Rachel Moran — *Interracial Intimacy: The Regulation of Race and Romance.* Chicago: University of Chicago Press, 2001.

Phyl Newbeck — *Virginia Hasn't Always Been for Lovers: Interracial Marriage Bans and the Case of Richard and Mildred Loving.* Carbondale: Southern Illinois University Press, 2004.

Brenda Lane Richardson — *Guess Who's Coming to Dinner: Celebrating Interethnic, Interfaith and Interracial Relationships.* Berkeley, CA: Wildcat Canyon, 2000.

Charles F. Robinson — *Dangerous Liaisons: Sex and Love in the Segregated South.* Fayetteville: University of Arkansas Press, 2003.

Dugan Romano — *Intercultural Marriage: Promises and Pitfalls.* Yarmouth, ME: Intercultural, 2001.

Renee Christine Romano — *Race Mixing: Black-White Marriage in Postwar America.* Cambridge, MA: Harvard University Press, 2003.

Maria P.P. Root — *Love's Revolution: Racial Intermarriage.* Philadelphia: Temple University Press, 2001.

Peter Wallenstein   *Tell the Court I Love My Wife: Race, Marriage and Law: An American History*. New York: Palgrave Macmillan, 2002.

Periodicals

Tricia Capistrano   "Emil's Big Chance Leaves Me Uneasy," *Newsweek*, June 19, 2006.

Benedict Carey   "In-Laws in the Age of the Outsider," *New York Times*, December 18, 2005.

James Caryn   "When It Comes to Casting, Love Conquers Color," *New York Times*, March 31, 2005.

Lynette Clemetson   "Love Without Borders," *Newsweek*, September 18, 2000.

Ellis Cose and Allison Samuels   "The Black Gender Gap," *Newsweek*, March 3, 2003.

Dee DePass   "Looking for Mr. White," *Essence*, June 2006.

Audrey Edwards   "Bring Me Home a Black Girl," *Essence*, November 2002.

Regan Good   "Color Dynamics," *New York Times Magazine*, February 9, 2003.

David Greenberg   "The Incredible Staying Power of the Laws Against Interracial Marriage," *Slate*, June 15, 1999.

Hendrik Hertzberg   "Bad News for Bigots," *New Yorker*, March 13, 2000.

Felicia R. Lee — "Bridging a Divide," *New York Times*, April 30, 2000.

Aimee Liu — "The Quake That Toppled Taboos and Built a Family," *Los Angeles Times*, April 18, 2006.

Jim Lobe — "Interracial Marriages on the Increase," *New York Amsterdam News*, July 21, 2005.

Angie Henderson Moncada — "Becoming Mrs. Moncada," *Hispanic*, October 2003.

Mireya Navarro — "When You Contain Multitudes," *New York Times*, April 24, 2005.

Lynn Norment — "The Multiple Colors of Love," *Ebony*, April 2006.

Tim Padgett and Frank Sikora — "Color-Blind Love," *Time*, May 12, 2003.

Amy Sohn — "The Long-Distancers," *New York Magazine*, December 10, 2001.

Susan Straight — "We Are Still Family," *New York Times Magazine*, December 18, 2005.

Michael Switow — "Interracial Marriage Blossoms in Malaysia," *Christian Science Monitor*, February 9, 2005.

Neely Tucker — "Loving Day Recalls a Time When the Union of a Man and a Woman Was Banned," *Washington Post*, June 13, 2006.

USA Today Magazine (Society for the Advancement of Education) — "Interracial Marriages Common in Military," April 2004.

Teresa Watanabe — "Mixed-Race Asians Find Pride as Hapas," *Los Angeles Times*, June 11, 2006.

Patricia J. Williams — "Uncommon Ground," *Nation*, April 5, 2004.

Tami Zer and Sjifra Herschberg — "Weddings on the Front Line," *Maclean's*, October 27, 2003.

Index